Laraine Kilberney

CW01095398

Best Wishes

S. Pickersgill

# Thoughts

# from my

# Book of Life

by

**Sidney Pickersgill**
**MSNU**

First Printed 2012

Published by
Saturday Night Press Publications
England
snppbooks@gmail.com
www.snppbooks.com

ISBN 978 1 908 421 02 9

Printed by Lightning Source
www.lightningsource.com

# Dedication

To my wife, Joyce.
Without her encouragement this book
may never have been written
and acknowledging the saying
'behind every good man is a good woman'.

# *Acknowledgements*

This book reflects the teachings of my parents who taught by their example.

My gratitude goes to Gerald O'Hara for his help and advice in putting the book forward for publication.
My thanks go to Mrs Ann Harrison of Saturday Night Press who has made this book possible;
and finally, to my three sons and to my long-time friends, Karan and David for their support.

Publisher's Note:
We gratefully acknowledge the use of photographs on pages 20, 76, 128, 148 from www.dreamstime.com, Wakefield-Herne Twinning Group, National Geographic and www.freeimages.co.uk, respectively.
Clip Art courtesy of GSP.
The portrait, facing, and photographs on pages 98 and 113 are the property of the author.
All other photographs by Ann Harrison.

Sidney Pickersgill, MSNU

# Contents

# Poems, Verses & Quotations

# Foreword

"You are the light of the World. A city that is set
upon hill cannot be hid." This puzzling beatitude from
'The Sermon on the Mount' quoted in *Matthew V*
recently became clearer to me when considering the
work of Minister Sidney Pickersgill.

If we regard the mind of Man to be a potential 'light'
to others as an example, then the work done by Sid in
these pages is as a light to others, in so far as the
message of his writings and thoughts bring others to
think spiritually, creatively and materially then indeed,
Sid is as a light to the World.

Sid may also be regarded as a 'city on a hill'. We
develop an instinct to know that those who are sincere
will be known by who they are, how they conduct
themselves and by the inspiration of their example.
Such a person is Minister Sidney Pickersgill. His
spiritual nature cannot be hid because it shines through
and is apparent – "By their work you will know them."

The various pieces that follow cover a wide field of
human experience. Each was inspired from life and was
delivered as a philosophical talk in a Spiritualist
church. Only later, at the suggestion of someone who
had listened to him, and with the encouragement of his
wife Joyce, did Sid consider them worthy of being
written up for the benefit of others.

Each piece is advisory on how to live our life. How best to relate to others, how to enjoy life and how to become closer to God. They are in that sense a practical guide to living. The writings teach what is truly of value in this world and how to prepare for the next life that awaits us all. They are also, an invaluable resource for those looking for inspiration themselves in giving church services.

As the title suggests the book is in part auto-biographical. Many of the sections have been inspired by his family experiences and speak volumes for the happy childhood that he enjoyed. His father was a miner and money was short but the family enjoyed a rich spiritual life because they created such from their emotionally stable family life. Nature, the senses and the intuitive appreciation of a greater world that surrounded and informed them was the source of their inspiration.

*Memento Mori*, the old Latin phrase, saying 'Remember that you must die' we find is not, in these pages, something to be dreaded. On the contrary in learning to love life, Sid's writings gently inspire us to live and learn to the full and to be an inspiration to others.

I feel honoured to be able to contribute to the publication of these 'down to earth' teachings.

Gerald O'Hara B.Sc.

# The Book of Life

Putting pen to paper was the last thing I had thought of but after a service at Wakefield church, a young man approached me and asked: "Do you write down what you have said?" I replied: "No, I am inspired by the spirit." He went on to say that it was a waste of spirit's time if what had been said was not recorded – it should be written down and retained for the future. "I cannot read or write." he said, "People are my books. Everyone has a story to tell. I read their body language." On leaving he added, "Next time you are taking a service, prepare it first."

When I was inspired to write my first church service, I thought I must try to satisfy my usual congregation of listeners and at the same time realise that there may be others listening who were new, so I endeavoured to find a simple way of expressing a spiritual meaning, through earthly things.

So my book of inspiration was born. The first piece (following this) was written in 1987. Many of the short pieces were witten between 1990-99 and published in the SNU's North Yorkshire District Council's magazine, *Link up* under 'What's cooking?'

But time waits for no man. Here we are in 2011 and time for me to share with you some thoughts from my Book of Life.

– Love and Sunshine

Sid.

# Chapters in our life

Have you ever thought of yourself as a book?

Sometimes I look back in my life and read my life's story. The different chapters make for good reading. Right now you are writing a chapter in your book of life; maybe this chapter is a love story, full of happiness and not enough time to pursue this wonderful part of life's story.

Others will be living a life of fear, for many people in this world live in fear and many people are putting into words the anguish of war, for it seems that war is natural to man – and there will always be wars.

Someone right now will be writing their chapter on solitude, so alone in the world, and just maybe, in the silence of solitude the best thoughts arise. Most of us may never know the blessing that silence can bring, and blindly pursue their path through life without tasting the joy of true silence – for it is said that silence is golden.

Some others will be writing about a life of good health and living long and happily; whilst another who does not enjoy good health and suffers pain and anxiety, may long to pass out of this world which they feel has brought them pain and sorrow .

A chapter in your book could include sorrow and pain for in some ways they are related. This chapter would probably include death, for death brings sorrow and pain, which may lead on to a chapter on thought, for when we experience a passing our thoughts become active and we ask many questions – without thought nothing could be accomplished.

All works of mankind are fruits, where thoughts are the seeds and, as in nature, each is true in its kind and the fruits from your seeds of thoughts will be so in like manner.

There are chapters in the book about right and wrong and this could be the longest chapter in the book. Men who have interests write about them especially about their experiences – for example fishing and the tall stories of the big one that got away.

Athletes may tell of the endurance and fitness and the way to win. In all team-sports they tell you that team-work always wins through. We could bring team-work into other chapters of our book. In team-work we support each other. If we don't, then we let the side down.

At this moment someone somewhere will be living a chapter on crime. It maybe just something small to begin with but it gets out of hand and in an effort not to be caught may kill to escape. Crime comes in many ways; crimes of passion are high on the list. Jealousy has been the result of many deaths and when a person has been imprisoned they live another chapter in the book of life.

A new chapter is of opportunities and progress and the real benefits missed at the time presented, if we failed to grasp the opportunity offered. How many times have you looked back in your life and said, if only I had done this or that my life would have been different?

Another chapter which is well written is a chapter on worry. We all worry about something or other – many times unnecessary worrying brings all kinds of illness and sometimes despair that puts an end to an earthly life.

The next chapter could contain the presence of wrong doing, of cruelty, an apparent injustice which impregnates the ways of mankind and gives rise to asking: "Why it is so?" – "Why is it allowed?"– "Why does man have the power to make others suffer?" Animals also suffer at the hands of man, so why is such misery allowed? If there is a supreme being over all, with unlimited power, why do people and animals have to suffer cruelty? Why is it not wiped away in one stroke by the Almighty. Such reasoning at first glance seems valid, but can we blame the Almighty for man's doings.

Some people will include in their book a chapter about service and the many ways to serve mankind. Doctors, nurses who care for the sick; those who work in the raising of monies for the many charities. Service is a way of giving; we all have something to give, a helping hand, a kindness, encouragement, a smile.

The world is featured in our book; people who live in rich exorbitant luxury and millions in extreme poverty; some in freedom while others have their freedom suppressed. The ways of the world are in grievous extremities. Its people are in need of a truth. Mankind is groping for an anchor to hold fast to from the storms of doubt and unrest, which appear to be gathering to engulf and destroy us all.

Now we have a chapter which contains peace. There is a need for peace in industry, in the home, in religion, and within ourselves. A reward is given to those who make peace – they will be called the children of God.

The book is sure to have a chapter in it about rich and poor. Many, by means of their possessions, have accumulated and surrounded their lives with an abundance, pleasing to the eye to the envy of their poorer brethren. It is said that there is one book for the rich and another for the poor and I expect they both make for good reading.

There are stories in the book telling of the many pleasures to be enjoyed but all life is intermingled with difficulties. Not all days are passed in sunshine because we have to experience the storms of life. One day you will review the book of your life and you will have a story to tell.

Men and women who have had a good life and write their autobiography will find that the true autobiography is still not completed when the body dies and the spirit returns.

At sometime in our life we may add a chapter in our book about prayer, a supplication or a thanksgiving from the heart to the highest power – the chapter of prayer never ends.

The book of life is a great adventure which allows us to explore uncharted places with hills to surmount and mountains to climb; to look back at your efforts with pride. In all of us there is a spirit of adventure which urges us at times to break away from dull routine and search for pastures new. Our life is one long adventure and there are many who vainly seek to obtain complete happiness by way of material things. In their misguided zeal, they should know their reward must be a bitter disappointment and empty of attainment.

The gateway of joy is not garnished with jewels and set apart for the favoured few. It is above price. Happiness cannot be bought. The secret of happiness is sought by many but found by few of those whose lives are devoted to material riches with the thought that they will bring perfect joy.

Now we might add a few words about loneliness to all who are tested – and many are. It would be a great comfort to know that there is much in the great scheme of life to gladden and lighten the gloom. Maybe your path is enshrouded in loneliness and despair but such is not intended by God. The earthly life at its best is but a drop when likened to the ocean's reserve in the true life to come.

The book will have to be left unfinished at the end of this life, but the happiness of all earthly life is ever dependent on the co-operation with the spirit world. And until this is universally acknowledged and effected there cannot be lasting joy or the life of humanity progressing as intended.

As we put together the chapters of our book everyone has been writing his or her own autobiography. It is up to you as to what title goes on the front of the book, whether it will be a good or a bad book is up to you – for life on this earth is comparatively short. Every fleeting second is of such importance and precious to all – as in the present sowing so, in justice, the future reaping will be. The fruits of all daily actions are being garnered and will themselves praise or condemn when the body is finally vacated.

*....as my father opened the gate to enter the meadow, it was just like being admitted to a new world.*

# Childhood

As a boy my mother and father took my two sisters and me for long walks, especially on Sunday evenings after church. As my father worked nights during the week, weekends were family days and we were lucky to be able to go on to farmland and meadows that belonged to the family. I remember, as my father opened the gate to enter the meadow, it was just like being admitted to a new world.

In bewitching loveliness, magic was in the air, the grass whispered as the breeze blew through it. As the breeze eased there was a solemn hush which seemed to fall over the whole field and everything in it. In a way it was a strange experience – everything became still, as if your whole being was caught up in rapturous feelings to behold the beauty of God. It was as if God had brought you to this place in order to say things to you in the silence that at any other time you would not stay to hear.

Is it not true that our lives are so rushed and hectic and we live at such a speed, that God has very little time to make himself heard above all the noise surrounding us today.

We are so hurried and rushed that we are as it were 'closed down' on all other wave-lengths and so we miss that still small voice when it calls. We have to extend our wave-length to receive the voice of the spirit when it makes contact.

I again remember being alone with dad as I sat on the gate; the evening sun disappearing, taking away the shadows. In some ways it was a strange experience, something that man cannot plan. It was at that moment – the soul's exaltation. I try to go back in time and thought to reproduce that feeling of what I believe to have been an uplifting moment brought by the spirit.

Now all this has an immense bearing on the question whether life is a good or a bad thing. So, if 'materially good' is the aim of our life let us cynically plan our lives accordingly.

But if the whole universe exists for spiritual ends obviously the only good is that which secures those ends. Our whole life seems to be set in securing the 'good things' in life and in doing so we miss many golden moments.

If you ask is life a good thing? You could say good for what? My father was a coal miner who worked long hours under-ground, often lying prone in a very limited space. I did join him for a short time and watched him working at the coal face in dust, noise, heat, and darkness. Not a good thing in itself but it gave me a further closeness and an understanding why he had a need for a daily walk in the country side. As I said in the beginning he was from farming roots but I suppose that also was hard work. He did plough the land with horses and in the same way, toil and sweat. The task of forcing that immense blade through the ground was not an easy one. We might ask what's the point. I suppose the outcome is something that comes afterwards – like the harvest.

So is life good? Maybe not all the time. It has its rare moments, as in the darkness of the mine, there was sometimes a glimmer of light.

I read there are two ways of working your way through life. The first is to stop thinking; the second is to stop and think. Some will try it one way and some the other. If we try the first way we may never achieve anything. It is better to take time and think; look life in the face, study, be silent, make time to listen. Faith insists that in fact that is what God does.

As man ploughs and mines, something beyond himself helps to build up the character – such an amazingly wonderful thing that can enter into communion with the divine. It is only in the light of the theme that I have tried to work out and understand the inward realisation of some words spoken to me many years ago by someone who is still very near and dear to me.

I love the familiar story of Michelangelo, when walking through a builder's yard, noticed in a corner a mis-shapen block of rough marble. The builder said it was useless.

Michelangelo said: "It is certainly not useless. Send it to my studio." The builder asked: "What will you do with it?" He answered: "There is an angel imprisoned within it and I must set it free."

I see my father's coal-blackened face and know that when it was washed it realised the hidden beauty of an angel.

The hymn says – *The voice of an angel falls sweet on our ears* and with the memory came the thought that there is no more quality in any of the greatest saints that is not present in everyone here today.

I was privileged in my early years to have parents who spent time with us, which gave me a chance to know them. I remember Dad saying to us that he could see something that we could not see and that we could see something that he could not see. Of course it was the other's eyes – the windows of the soul; no one can see their own eyes – only the reflections.

Have you ever looked in the mirror and wondered who that good-looking person is? For we see only what we want to see. I suppose we often look at ourselves through rose-coloured spectacles. A young man sees himself as a fair decent chap maybe even attractive. I have never looked any different! We see ourselves as anything we want to be. Shakespeare's Hamlet says: *This above all, to thine own self be true.* You yourself are *not* a body functioning in time, you are a spirit functioning in the eternal. You are not a creature of time to whom time can do anything deadly. You are a spirit making use of time, imprisoned for a while in time's limitation, waiting to be freed – but you belong to the timeless.

If a man moves from a suburb into the 'real' life of a city, you might be disappointed because you could not have physical converse with him, but you would not be saddened beyond the normal sadness of physical separation and when man dies he has only gone from the suburbs of time to live in the eternal city.

Before I close the gate I must just go back into the field and gather a small bunch of wild flowers. These would have been taken home for Mum. Tonight I am sure she will share them with my two sisters – milkmaids, cowslips, buttercups – the gold and violet – my favourite colours.

# Shoe-shine boy

I started my working life at the age of fourteen in a shoe factory as an apprentice clicker, someone who cuts out the shoe uppers. Being a small factory meant that we made all kinds of footwear clogs, heavy working boots, sport shoes, golf shoes, football and rugby boots.

I have worked in factories that made high-class ladies' and gents' footwear and those who specialised in dancing shoes – all needing special attention to help those who wore them to perform better.

You may not realise that we always worked a season in front, in summer we would be preparing for the winter and visa versa.

All the ladies waited for the spring sales and became excited as they waited for the new styles that would be introduced. Each new season the ladies would be trying on all the new footwear to find a pair that was comfortable – lucky were those who found a perfect fit.

I remember the first time my children were introduced to wearing shoes – they did not take it lightly – they did their best to keep their feet free. I am sure all of you love to sit down, kick off your shoes and put your feet up.

I wonder how many miles my feet have carried me?

Many songs have been written about walking. One said – *These boots were made for walking* and another *Walking back to happiness* – that one went down well in the Eurovision contest. Yet another said – *I'll walk with God from this day on* but the one that I like best is the oldest and says – *I'll walk beside you through the world today.* This message should be reassuring, for the song tells us that our loved ones are always beside us through cloud and sunshine, and will walk with us into the future.

It's amazing how God equips us for every season in our life; he is our support and guidance in every step we take on life's highway.

At a time when we least expect it we feel that we are walking on air. This is the time when God carries us through a difficult situation and smoothes the rough road that hinders our progression.

We must remember at all times that we are walking back to where we set out from. Your pathway through life may take you in many different directions until you find the right way to take. God wants to equip us with new visions. He wants us to walk with confidence, scaling every obstacle along life's way. This is the time to put on your working boots and get mobile and work relentlessly in the service of your God; stride out with confidence and let others know that there is no death.

We all constantly walk out of one situation into another and many times we feel depressed and let down. We feel abandoned, but who knows, what happened may turn out to be the best thing for our future, for many times happiness comes out of a disaster.

With each new season comes changes – a casting off and a changing scene. At this moment you may be in the springtime of your life but always remember winter is never far away and we must prepare for it. New adventures will only be exciting if we do not carry mud on our shoes from the past. It takes courage to walk away from the past, forgetting failure habits and memories that hamper our progression.

My father always said that you can learn a lot about a man by the shoes he wears. I can see him now, singing the song – *Shoeshine boy got no time to play,* as he cleaned the family shoes, taking away the dullness and shining them until you could see your face in them. I suppose the song – *Following in father's footsteps, following dear old dad* is appropriate here for I still use the brushes to bring a shine to my shoes and I take this job very seriously, for we can never overestimate the importance of life's good habits, they lead to our growth of character.

All your experiences bring the gifts of your life into service. Not only to use well the gifts that you have now at work but to develop what you have into greater skills and power of service.

Do not allow your spiritual powers to rest; keep them maintained and ready for use so that when you are called to work for the greater spirit you can step out with a firm tread and receive new lessons in life with every new experience.

Every new piece of knowledge, should be accepted – not to keep – but to minister in dispensing the gifts of the spirit. There is something in this message which speaks of a deep feeling of peace.

The fact that there are new religious ideas coming forward with new beliefs it is difficult to find a philosophy for life in a world of such mixed beliefs. This is where Spiritualists can help. Our philosophy is a way of life – for living – and for dying. The vision on earth is never full and clear but it grows brighter and brighter as we walk ever towards the light.

I feel that a philosophy of life comes through thoughts and experiences. We all have these moments in life when we have direct experiences of a deeper reality than we are normally conscious of. This then sets our thoughts in action. We know that thoughts are living things and can be used for good or bad.

I have just read an article in a magazine, which asked if science could be a substitute for religion. It is reassuring to know that Spiritualism embraces, Science, Philosophy, and Religion. Nevertheless Spiritualism is receiving more respect than it did some fifty years ago. I have lived to see discussions, which would have been impossible in the past, as topics of conversation especially on television programmes, which demonstrates that nothing that the sceptics have said or the scientists discovered has disproved the claims of Spiritualism.

Our future in this life, and in the next, depends on ourselves alone. The fruits from your sowing will be gathered when you leave this world and will determine your status in the world of spirit. Follow your Heavenly Father's footsteps. He will lead you in the right direction; he will keep you from falling and your feet from wandering if you stumble; comfort your weary feet as you travel the rough pathways of life. With such a promise as this, we can run or walk through our lives knowing that we are being guided and guarded.

As for shoes, they are essential in our lives, to protect our feet in every activity we wish to undertake. So put your best foot forward, with head erect and shoulders square, live for today. Stand on your own two feet. If you do not expect anything from anyone you cannot be disappointed. Always place yourself in harmony with spirit, for God gave you eyes to see them and lips that you may tell.

Witness the power of the spirit, when you dwell on the song sung by Gerry Marsden of Gerry and the PaceMakers and adopted by Liverpool football club. They tell us that we'll *Never Walk Alone*. When the fans raise their voices as one you can feel the power transcending.

Walk on, with hope in your hearts for you know that you will always have your loved ones close at hand. Rejoice in the knowledge that you will never walk alone.

# They call me a dreamer

They call me a dreamer – well maybe I am. Not that I am a person who has his head high in the clouds all the time, but at times I am sure you will agree its not a bad idea, to dream and to escape from reality of material situations. Most days we have a grumble but move on, hoping things will get better but as we get older, we look back, to those very days with nostalgia.

It is said that the grass is greener on the other side of the fence and it may be true that many things look a lot better from a distance than they are. It is not until you are in the so-called greener grass that the problems begin to appear and the reality of the situation comes to light.

We are told to live for today, the past is gone and is a memory; the future is yet to be and we should live in the present. Remember – it is God's gift to you, that is why it is called the 'present'. It may well be that it is better to live now and let tomorrow take care of its self.

One thing is pretty certain, and that is probably, the only advantage of growing old is that one is able to benefit from the experience of life. The trouble is by that time of life a person may be too tired to bother, but it would be true to say that those who get most out of life are those who put the most into it.

Life should mean far more than many of us ever dream of. It is not merely passing through this earth life with all the comforts, – enough food to sustain the body and clothes to keep us warm. Life on earth means that we should strive to bring into our lives the God-like image.

We need never be anxious about our tasks in life, for every common walk of life is glorious, with the God-presence. We need never be anxious about our mission. If you want to know God's plan for you, do his will each day and if there is a larger task or some other duty to perform, he will lead you in that direction.

The hardest school tasks are easily mastered in comparison with the lessons of patience, calm temper, forgiveness, unselfishness, humility, contentment. Even at best we learn these lessons, but slowly. We must not measure by earthly standards when testing the failure or success of life.

There are lives which the world rates as successful, but in the after-life rate as failures. Then others over which men drop a tear of pity, are put down in God's sight as a noble success. Your labour for God is never in vain, then the real measure of our wealth, is what will be ours in eternity.

The old water wheel runs around and around outside the mill. It seems to be accomplishing nothing, the shaft holding it goes through the wall, and turns the machinery inside, Making flour to feed the hunger of many, or driving spindles that weave beautiful fabrics. In some ways our lives may seem, with all their activities to be leaving no results, but they reach into the unseen; and who knows what blessings they become, what impressions they leave on other lives on into eternity.

So if we want progress in our lives, we must practise the art of loving, this would go towards making world peace. In this way your life would become happy and once you have created happiness remember you created that happiness through the greater power of the spirit, as a gift to give to others.

As we open ourselves up to the inflow of the Great Spirit, we will be benefited with the gifts of the spirit, and just as a plant grows slowly but steadily, so do the gifts that have been allotted to you. Everyone possesses a wonderful degree of recuperative power. It is so natural we may overlook it but those who recognise the wonderful allotted gift, realize the greatness of the spirit at work through them.

But all this requires practice and patience, there is no easy road to its accomplishment, so practise your gift whenever you get the opportunity and you will gradually begin to realise what a good thing you have been missing all these years.

As I see it, our function is to demonstrate that there is a life force and to spread the word that there is survival of death. We must encourage others to walk along the way that is shown, and to discover spiritual truths for themselves.

As we go through life most of us experience emotion, which also occurs during our work-a-day experiences or we may find that some situations are put there for us to work out and understand. Hopefully we will learn from them, gain knowledge and store it until we need to draw on it when required to help and comfort our fellow man.

It is hard when someone we love, through whatever condition passes into spirit. Only those who have experienced it can know what it is like – the loneliness – the sense of emptiness – the love we feel we've lost.

But remember this, the love that they had for us does not die, love is the link between this life and the life hereafter and cannot be broken by death. How long this earthly journey may last, we do not know – but how comforting to know that our loved ones who have gone before, will be waiting for us.

\* \* \* \* \*

*In God's Hands*

*Here is a book of chapters three,*
*The past, the present and the yet to be,*
*The past we know, is put away,*
*The present we're living, day by day,*
*But the third and the last*
*Of these chapters three*
*Is in God's hands,*
*He holds the key.*

(Author unknown)

# A still small voice

As I grew up my parents would say to my sisters and me that, as we travelled through life, there would be many things calling for our attention, some good, some bad, so we must listen to that still small voice within, which guides us to make the right decisions.

My mother, God bless her, is never far away, for whenever I have a doubt in my mind, I hear her voice and realise how she influenced and shaped my life. She always had little quotes, such as – *The gold in any religion will only become valuable when the impurities have been removed from it.* You have to first discern the gifts of the spirit, use every gift that comes from the spirit and realise that this will not mean the doors will automatically open and you will rise to the top. Your performance depends on your commitment to practice. You can only use the gifts of the spirit well if you practise in the same manner, for constant good practice leads to constantly good development.

We all know that in order for us to become a master of any craft or discipline, we have to give our time over to practise, practise and more practise, if we want to accomplish perfection.

Remember confidence is contagious, if parents show confidence, it is picked up by their children. You can also pass it on in friendships and you can become an influence to all around you.

Remember God created the characteristics that made you unique.

When a child is born everything in the family changes. The same is true for you when you give birth to what the spirit placed within you. Do you realise that before you were born plans for your earthly life had already been decided? God gave you freewill so the choice is yours. You have been picked for a purpose – a large investment has been placed on you, so why should you not repay the loan with interest. This earthly life of ours is on loan and one day the loan will have to be repaid.

Once when doing my household chores, – something I do not enjoy, but I know that they have to be done, and when they are all complete, I can relax and enjoy the fruits of my labour – I was 'hoovering' the sitting room when I found a piece of a jigsaw puzzle. I was tempted to throw it away, but realised if I did, it would mean that without this small piece the rest of the puzzle would be incomplete and that they would also end up in the rubbish bin.

The small piece could resemble you or me, for we are just a small piece of a larger picture waiting to take our place.

So the small pieces have to be taken care of so we can complete the picture. It made me think how our lives are made up of bits and pieces and it takes all our strength to keep our eyes focussed, for they are the most influential part of the body. We must not let our selves crave everything our eyes see – and our ears must be trained to listen carefully for that still small voice when it calls.

Keep your feet walking on a spiritual pathway and remember – let the truth alone be spoken, for it is a well known fact that those people who grow through a crisis, learn which hopes, dreams and expectations were violated by the event. They identify where repair work is needed and develop a way of life for the future. At first you may feel that nothing will ever be the same again, but it encourages you to reach within yourself to find hidden strength, which you did not know existed.

Then with the help of those spirit friends you will succeed in what you were called to do; to use your physical body to help those around you, because the time will come when you may need help from others. Help is not to impose; it is to support, without asking for personal recognition and you benefit by becoming enlightened and finding happiness in service rendered.

You may not acquire immediate benefits during your earthly experience, your reward will be that eternal happiness which is a supreme achievement and remember you only become what you are prepared to become. People, who fail to make the most of their opportunities or follow their impressions, will as the Rolling Stones' song says – *Get no satisfaction.*

It may seem no matter how much we try we do not manage to get any satisfaction, but maybe we are looking for it in the wrong place, when the true source of satisfaction is right under our noses and we fail to recognise it, because we are trying so hard to obtain it on our own, instead of listening to that still small voice.

Listening maybe the most loving thing you do today, especially if you take time to listen to someone's troubles. This may lead on to the subject of life after death and knowing this takes away some of the fear and pain connected with it. The phrase that someone has 'been called to higher service' expresses the idea that there is a reward for services rendered in earthly life. A hymn in the Spiritualist National Union hymn book (No. 231 by R. Driver) says:

> Listen to the angel message,
> Sent from heaven above,
> Breathing words of joy and comfort,
> And of love.
>
> Truth in dazzling radiance streaming
> Through the midnight gloom,
> Now has pierced the sombre shadows
> Of the tomb.
>
> Loved ones who have crossed the border
> Send us words of cheer,
> Telling that they guard and guide us;
> Ever near.
>
> And that he who nobly striveth
> Here to bless mankind,
> There in sweet congenial labour
> Heaven shall find.
>
> Unto him, whose loving kindness
> Orders all thy ways,
> Lift thine heart in glad thanksgiving,
> And in praise.

In the light of this knowledge, there should not be the slightest doubt in your heart. Open your ears, the answer can then be spoken.

# Change your thinking

The word 'change' is used all the way through our life. We all change as we grow older. We change our appearance, our character, our clothes. We live in a world of change.

We are told from all sides, that changes are needed in all walks of life for, by man's greed, with the destruction of the rain forests and the plundering of the earth and sea, 'an atmosphere of doom has encircled the earth'. But we wonder, will it be for the better?

However, unless we accept the challenge of change, we will never know. All around us things are changing and while change may not suit everyone, it is inevitable. Don't let it scare you. We can help in the most natural way, by a change of attitude. Try a new approach and purify and lift the thoughts you transmit.

Watch the change within you and you will bring a new light into this world which is dying around us.

Peace can come and selfishness disappear – misery will turn to joy and all who are denied that which is necessary for their sustenance will be able to live in the kingdom of heaven on earth.

# What can God do?

Hold a rose in your hand and look at what God created. Climb a hill and let your eyes rest on the view; take a walk in the park or garden or beside a singing stream; take a moment to be quiet, to think, to pray, to dream.

If your thoughts are centred on earthly things you will forget that life is bigger than what materialistic living brings. Do not lose sight of what is real.

The good and lovely things, the caring and sharing, the doing of things that help and heal a hurt or ease a load. Kind thoughts bring harmony and we are comforted in the knowledge that there is never an end to life in God and yet we cannot expect that things will always remain the same. But in the changing conditions and circumstances in the world, or in our individual lives, we can be sure of eternal verities. Amid the changing opinions and attitudes the unchanging wisdom of God is always with us to reveal the right way and his love is the key that will open all doors.

We must remember that every day is part of our journey in life. Each day we have a choice of the way we take; each day through prayer we can find the guidance and direction we need.

There are many travellers on the highway of life, who stay in the fast lane and leave others behind, without any consideration.

What we must realise is that we cannot continue to travel this way; we must slow down and remember others who might need help, although it may upset and delay our own plans.

Each day we can carry with us thoughts and attitudes that are positive. Whatever is before us, let us prepare the way.

This poem – author unknown was taken from a book titled *Awake My Heart*:

*"A commonplace life," we say, and we sigh;*
*Yet why should we sigh as we say?*
*The commonplace sun in the commonplace sky*
*Makes lovely the commonplace day.*

*The moon and the stars, are commonplace things,*
*The flowers that bloom and the robin that sings;*
*Yet sad were the world and unhappy our lot,*
*If flowers all failed and the sunshine came not!*
*And God, who considers each separate soul,*
*From commonplace lives, makes a beautiful whole.*

# A way of life

Spiritualist philosophy takes away the fear of death and it takes away the fears in this life. There are just as many people afraid of this life and for their future in this world, as there are those afraid of Spiritualism. It is not just another religion. It is the basis of all religions. If we did not believe in life after death and in God, as all religions teach, then there would be no point in any religion.

Spiritualism helps us to understand that our lives have a purpose and teaches us how to live our lives. We must understand that our philosophy is a way of life and not just a vehicle for message seekers.

It teaches us about the power of the mind and thoughts and through them how to work out our own salvation. Our religion teaches us to know our own power and build up good habits and eradicate bad ones – or it should. So few people understand the power of thought and still fewer about the power within each one of us.

Once we realise this power within, not only those with the gift of clairvoyance etc, but the power of our own individual thoughts, we come to know that we are creating our own future here and now. Thoughts are living forces and it is of paramount importance that we endeavour, always, to control our thoughts.

We constantly send out thoughts that enter other peoples' minds, attracting more like-thoughts and as we send out so they come back re-inforced. Therefore when we broadcast thoughts of anger, hate, or jealousy, they come back. When thoughts of love, peace, and goodwill are sent out they return to us, threefold and sometimes more. It comes down to this – 'as we think, so we are' – the more love we give out the more will return and more peaceful we shall be.

'As we sow so shall we reap'. I am a firm believer in karma, the law of cause and effect. Not only in this life on earth, but also in the spirit world, to which we shall all return. So in a nutshell, if we want love we must give love. If we want success we must think it. If we want good health, we must think good health, even when we don't feel well and if you want friendship, then you must be a friend. It is so simple – as are all God's laws – so easy to understand and carry out.

Always remember that we are creating our heaven or hell now by our persistent thoughts. Heaven and hell are states of consciousness, which are of now. We do not have to pass to the world of spirit to experience them. We are creating them now by the way we think with our daily thoughts.

While we are on the subject of the spirit world, we should keep in mind that we are creating now the kind of spiritual home we shall have, by the way we live and act while on earth. Thought, that great creative power, is, after Love, the greatest asset that man possesses and hand-in-hand these two powers are capable of changing the whole world.

They could, if rightly used, turn the earth into heaven but instead man is often too busy trying to turn it into hell. Thought power in its many expressions can be used for good or evil and whilst the free-will granted to man has given him the power to choose the use he will make of it, fortunately there are many who today are beginning to realise what can be accomplished with this power and are using it for good.

Spiritual healing is one amongst many things which can be accomplished. Thought and Love power hand-in-hand, united, is very necessary in the healing process. All God-given powers such as love, thought, music, colour, are each a study in themselves and can blend together. God has given these gifts to man but he must be open and ready to receive and make good use of them.

I think of people as notes of music. When in tune with one another they bring sweet music and harmony. One person can bring discord, if they are out of tune with those around them.

Life on Earth is a school and we must pass through all kinds of classrooms. To my mind, you and I may have to pass through many lives in order to acquire the required knowledge. If in some way our progression is hampered then it follows we shall have to make a return journey to complete our task but whatever happens to you, try to feel that it's just one more step on your journey home.

Life for most of us is a very mixed experience it includes good and bad times. Love and laughter are mingled with sorrow and pain. Unless we have known all these things, can we say we have lived? We all know that life is full of ups and downs and of course we dislike and resent the downs. Yet, the 'downs' maybe much more valuable to us than the 'ups' – if we learn how to handle them.

We cannot choose what life will bring to us. We have to take life as it comes. Yet could I preach this in a hospital ward? Would it be a comfort for patients with an incurable disease? I don't think it would. Could it reconcile a man to the agony of a broken back when he found himself under a fall of coal or a stone in a mine? I can see and understand what meaning – other than sheer bitterness – it could have for his wife.

It is not God who does things like this. If he did we would see God as a God of cruelty not of love. There are many people suffering in hospitals and in other conditions throughout the world, but God is at work there – doing his best to restore and revitalise many back to good health again.

No religion promises its followers happiness and prosperity to all who follow it. What happens to us is not of God's making but that of our own. I do not say that God does not take a hand in our affairs. On the contrary, his guiding and protecting hand is always showing and pointing us the way but this does not mean he will always guide us away from hardship or that he will protect us from all pain. I believe he guides us continually through hardship and pain, to a destiny that is ours. I am sure, if we have faith enough to co-operate with him, he will use hardships and pain to educate us in his own essential goodness.

Whatever happens to us in our lives nothing can hurt us in ourselves if we live a life of faith. If we really believe that then we can take life as it comes and not be afraid of it.

Indeed by the grace of God there is nothing in this world that we need be afraid of – except ourselves.

(written in 1992)

# Memories

For the past six or seven years, my wife Joyce and I have seen the old year out and the new year in at our local hotel. We sat in the same seats as last year and we were joined by the same people who sat with us on New Year's Eve in 1991. A remark was passed that: "It is as if we have been here all the time." – as if time had stood still. We all agreed time does not go by slowly any more and we get older without realising what is happening to us.

We all had plenty to say about our younger days. Those were the 'golden days' – never to come again. What cricketers there were in those days, such strokes and such mighty hits! No footballer could distribute the ball as in our days; to play the game one had to be tough; we had a leather ball to head, not one these light plastic ones.

The old actors – well they could act. The films today have no stories to tell.

We were sitting in what was once the church vicarage, now a hotel. Our friends remembered the vicar who had lived there – "He could preach a good sermon." they said, "If only we could hear sermons like his again." I am sure no one would begrudge us our golden memories, growing more and more colourful as we came to the witching hour.

A new year comes. What lies ahead? There is an old saying that the future never lies ahead of us but creeps up on us from behind. The essential truth of this is the fact that we always make our future before we live it. The problems of today are not the products of today. They represent the thoughts and choices of yesterday.

So we awaken the sleeping memories of the past and come across the incident that left so deep a mark upon us. We look back and wonder what will the new year provide for us. No sooner had we wished each other a Happy New Year, when the news flashed across the across the world, another person killed in Ireland; fighting continued in Yugoslavia – nothing had changed.

It comes down to this, among things that may happen at any moment, on any day, there may lurk something that is marked with destiny. Our chances of happiness and usefulness in the future come and peep at us. They take us unaware, when we are off guard.

I do wish at this season of the year, when we go around buying expensive things, everyone would stop for a moment and think of the many others who are fighting for mere existence. Life for most of us is of very mixed experience – it includes rainy days as well as sunny days. Love, laughter and labour are in it, so are sorrow and pain.

Unless we have known all these things and more, can we say we have lived?

I wish you a Happy New Year!

# Laughter

My favourite programmes on television are word games, especially *Count Down*. I learn a new word every day. The English language, I think, is the hardest to learn and no wonder, when so many words have two meanings. I remember as a young boy the word 'laugh' presented a problem when it came to spelling, just looking at it brings a smile to my face.

My father use to say: "If you haven't got a smile I will give you one of mine." Years later at work I remember one of the ladies who was having a bad day, and everyone was keeping their distance, so I quoted my father's words. She smiled and went on her way. Many times afterwards she would say to me: "I've given someone a smile," and we would laugh together.

Laughter is a great healer. Anyone who has the gift of creating laughter is truly blessed; they are never alone, attracting others to them. "Laugh and the world laughs with you," we say but sometimes it's hard to let oneself go. What joy it is to go on holiday. Cares drop away, we feel free. I have a good laugh when I change into my shorts.

A few years ago my wife Joyce and I stayed with friends in Porthcawl. They had two young children (young ladies now). One day we were out for a walk when suddenly the rain came down. We had taken our umbrellas, so it did not matter. Everyone was dashing for shelter, but we were having a good time. The children were performing in the musical, *Singing in the Rain* so we practised going along the street dancing and singing, twirling our brollies, much to the amusement of passers-by.

Visiting the seaside shows are always an uplifting experience. Corny jokes perhaps but how much better one feels having a good laugh; trying to remember the jokes to pass on and bring a smile to someone's face.

A young mother brought her baby to see us. I did enjoy the little fellow chuckling away. In the end everyone around joined in the laughter. Such was the reaction brought about by this small mouth.

Which brings me back to *Count Down* when Sheila Ferguson of *The Three Degrees* was the visitor. She had a lovely smile belonging to a generously proportioned mouth. A vivacious person who lit up the programme. As I write this, the song – *When you're smiling, keep on smiling, the whole world smiles with you,* keeps popping into my mind.

In a health magazine, which I brought back from back from America, is an article written by a member of *The Laughing Clubs of India.* It says: "A daily dose of laughter is good medicine, for it can lower the blood pressure, combat stress, boost your immune system and give you energy."

Also, in a *Saga* magazine, I read that a G.P. from Stockport, has collected jokes throughout his career. He has had his book on medical jokes published titled: *Laughter is good for Health.* His book is as popular as his prescriptions. He says: "Laughter brings more laughter and this brings better health."

# In tune

A friend of mine who plays the violin, tunes it to the piano.When he strikes the note on the piano, it causes the corresponding string of the violin to vibrate. Many people unfortunately have tuned themselves to the discordant notes of the world around them, and every time a note of discord is sounded they respond to it, 'vibrate' to it, pick it up and pass it on. If a note of sickness is struck in the world these people respond to it; when a note of fear is struck they cause panic by responding to it.

What we have to do is re-tune ourselves; to vibrate our good intentions. We must be attuned to the truth of the spirit. We must learn to harmonise with the idea of God. We must not be impressed by things of lesser value. We must start giving our attention to spiritual values in order that we can appreciate the higher values and develop our spiritual vision. The result will be that of opening ourselves up to spirit. It is through the medium of spiritual communion that all worth-while things are accomplished.

# Love

Reading a magazine I came across this: 'Love usually makes you weep more often than it makes you smile', but I remember another old saying – 'It is better to have loved and lost than to have never loved at all'.

Many songs have been written about love. The song voted 'the best ever' in one list was *Love makes the world go round* and now of course we have a musical called *Aspects of Love*. The song that I like best was sung by the 'Mills Brothers' (but they sounded like the 'Ink Spots') entitled *You always hurt the one you love*. This was a hit with the public and top of the hit parade for quite a while in 1944. I think the writer of these lyrics wrote them with feeling.

One of the oldest sayings about love is that 'true love never runs smooth' and there are many types of love. For instance, love between man and woman and this does not mean that they have to be joined together in matrimony. I love my sisters.

Then there is the love a mother has for her children, father and son, mother and daughter. The gardener loves his plants – how he cares for them. Some pet lovers go overboard and give their dog or cat lots of love and affection. A friend of mine always says that his wife thinks more about their dog than she does of him. Giving is also an expression of love.

Perhaps from a very early age we hear our parents saying to us: "If you are a good boy or girl, I'll love you." I remember sitting in the waiting room at the doctor's surgery, beside a young mother and her small daughter who was restless and a little naughty. Mum told her to behave, which had no effect but when mum said: "If you are naughty I won't love you." The little girl looked into her mother's eyes and said: "You do love me." Her mum did not answer and after three or four more times of asking said: "*Please*, Mum, say you love me."

We all waited. You could feel the tension in the air. A few moments passed, then the little girl said: "I will be good." Then mum said: "I love you." The song *Love Changes Everything* came to mind and it is impossible to put into words the love in that child's eyes.

My mother use to say to my sisters and me that God was watching us and that if we were naughty or did anything wrong a black mark would be put beside our names. I visualised all those black marks against my name with dismay and horror. To us our very survival depends on being loved and as children we modify our behaviour in order to be loved.

Because of love we often carry a heavy burden for long periods of time because we have a sense of duty to those we love. Children build up an effigy of perfection around parents, and it comes as a colossal dis-illusionment on discovering that parents are not the perfect specimens they imagine them to be.

Most people look upon love as a natural physical yearning like hunger that can easily be satisfied but love is not a physical thing. All fairy tales end with marriage and living 'happily ever after'. But marrying is just the first step and must be worked at.

Love is understanding, patient and kind, and it's the little deeds that mean a lot. The song says – *Touch her hair when you pass her chair. Say she looks nice when she's not.* The next line talks about diamonds and pearls so I think we will move on!

The longer I live, the clearer I see that love is an emotion of maturity. As I live in the rhythm and the harmony of spirit I find that my days are divinely ordered. I am filled with joy and love. I live in love with life and its infinite possibilities. In a sense love is everything. It is the key to life and its influences are those that move the world.

So we must live in the thought of love for all, and if we do you will draw love to you from all. Live in the thought of malice or hatred and they will come back to you like the boomerang. Remember love inspires love and hatred breeds hatred. A quotation I read said – *Tell me how much one loves, and I will tell you how much one has seen of God, the spirit of infinite love.*

There is a deep scientific principle that if you would have all the world love you, then you must love all the world. When someone treats us badly our thought is – how can we repay them. We can do this in their own coin but if you do then you yourself are sinking to the same level. You must rise above that and show yourself wiser by sending them love. We need more gentleness, sympathy and compassion in our common human life.

We, as Spiritualists, must be an example to others. Instead of looking to repay with malice, we must try to understand what has happened in their lives. We must look beyond the hard surface presented to us by the unhappy person and by showing sympathy and compassion it will change into love and love will manifest itself in kindly service.

When we on earth feel strongly about someone, we should ask ourselves: "What can I contribute to the relationship? Can I feel comfortable loving and happy within this relationship? Which values are important?" We have to have priorities, such as honesty, generosity, trust, peace of mind, openness, sharing, truthfulness, and some freedom. We should also have the same experience towards God who is the supreme power of love expressed.

Now experience this with me – imagine yourself relaxing on a beautiful sandy beach. The sand is warm and soft under your hands. Now grab a handful of sand and squeeze it tight. Notice what happens. It begins to slip through your clenched fist. The more you try to hold on to it, the faster it trickles through until it's all gone.

Now scoop up another handful of sand, but instead of making a tight fist leave your hand open and notice how the grains of sand remain there free to fall or remain. By doing this you find yourself holding the grains of sand in your hands for much longer with less effort and a lot less energy than if you had tried to possess them and hold them in your grip.

However has either way of being with the sand changed your feeling about it obviously it has not. You still think of it as worth experiencing and it is still as beautiful and fulfilling to sit there and enjoy the peacefulness and softness. Best of all it will still be there for you to enjoy again and again.

Life and love are much the same as those grains of sand. We want to possess for ever the feelings we have had aroused within us. We want to hold on to them and recapture those moments of the first excitement and the feeling of happiness when we fell in love.

So when we part from dear ones we must not hold on to them. We must allow them their freedom. Let them go – and in that way we shall keep them and, like the sand, we shall be able to enjoy them returning to us from time to time. For love is the almighty link between the two worlds.

I ask you to take the touch of love that God gives to you freely. For you are a part of God's creation. He made you in his likeness. You may not be aware of your spiritual heritage but God loves you. Let these words be written upon your mind and remember you do not have to measure up to anyone else.

The poem opposite was give to me by a lady at Keighley church. It was written by her husband, when on active service in the Second World War.

*Love is...*

*Love is a thing, which cannot be bought,*
*Love is a thing that should be taught,*
*Love is a thing that helps the distraught,*
*Love is a wonderful thing.*

*Love is a thing for fathers and mothers,*
*Love is a thing for sisters and brothers,*
*Love is a thing we should give to another,*
*Love is a beautiful thing.*

*Love is a thing for both strong and weak,*
*Love is a thing, of which we should speak,*
*Love is a thing we all should seek,*
*Love is a glorious thing.*

*Love is a thing for all mankind,*
*Love is a thing which has not declined,*
*Love is a thing for peace of mind*
*Love is the only thing.*

What more can I say – except
              "I just called to say – I love you."

# Prayer

sually anyone who feels that life is meaningless and without purpose sometimes, indeed often, turns to prayer.

Prayer helps to establish a person's faith and strengthens the will to find a meaning in life. I establish justice in my life, through prayer. I pray first that God will understand me and I ask for his guidance. I include others in my prayers. If some situation seems unjust, I pray that every one involved will find his or her perfect fulfilment. I pray for everyone to have understanding and guidance so that everyone will work together to bring harmony into the world.

I thank God for this moment before me. I give thanks for yesterday. I bless tomorrow but live for today.

Friends, thank God for all that you are, for there are many less fortunate than we are – those who are sick in body, mind and spirit; those who live in countries with governments who dictate and oppress freedom. There are many millions suffering hunger. They maybe separated by distance but prayer brings us closer.

I breathe a prayer of thanks that God's healing power is at work; that healing is taking place. If one's life needs direction and purpose I know that God can be trusted to make plain the way. And I know that the guiding light of spirit is always shining, revealing the right path.

So we pray for our loved ones, for those who are unhappy so that they can, through prayer, establish faith in God and find a new meaning in life.

As we pray for ourselves, for love and direction, new openings come. The productivity of our nature opens up with new thoughts about life and our part in it. We see then that prayer by prayer we can transform the pattern of our life.

We know that God is the spirit of wisdom and if we would take time each day to acknowledge the Great Spirit and quietly listen to its directions, we would emerge from our prayers relaxed and refreshed. Taking a few moments now and then brings our thoughts, feelings and emotions under control. We know that thoughts are living things and we must have order in our thoughts. With the power of prayer we are able to quell anxious thoughts and feelings and bring calm within us.

In prayer we place ourselves and all our longings in God's care. We turn our lives over to him and let his spirit move through us, inspiring and directing us.

There is another form of prayer which consists of repeating a certain form of words. Sometimes this repetition becomes meaningless. Now I say without any hesitation that every prayer is heard by God when we pray from the heart. Then something of the basic essence of our self goes into it. God's inspiration will flow to all human beings who make themselves available to receive it.

God wants a voice in this world. He longs to communicate to people of this world. He calls for channels of expression; for men and women who will continue his work. We expect God to listen to our prayers and to answer them but in our asking we fail to listen to the wishes of God.

Furthermore, when through prayer, he gives us what we desire, do we think how can we repay him? You know everything we need or use in this world has to be paid for, so why should we not repay God, for what he has done for us – with interest.

People often simply regard prayer as a way to ask, beg and plead for something. Many think of prayer as a one-way system, in that if we ask earnestly and persistently and long enough God will surely respond to our cry.

So what about our relationship with God? That is a question which we are inclined to shirk. Surely we need to build up a closer relationship and through prayer God does not remain a stranger for long. Knowing that we have the God-spirit with in us, the spirit of wisdom, we have a centre of peace to which we can always return.

In prayer we can place ourselves and all our desires and longings in God's care. What really matters now is that we find some way of praying that is real. We do not want time-wasting prayers – for we are all troubled by wandering thoughts. We must forget selfish prayers that begin, "Please, God, give me .." and instead say, "make me, show me, use me."

For it is in prayer we ask for renewed trust and stronger faith, for more tolerance and love, especially towards those who differ from ourselves.

I have always found prayer difficult. So often it seems like a fruitless game of hide and seek. I know that God is very patient with me, without that patience

I would be lost. Yet I cannot leave prayer alone for long. Soon my needs drive me to prayer.

Consider the story of the captains of two sailing-ships, stranded in port, waiting for a good strong wind to start their voyage home. One night, on retiring, they both sent out prayers, asking God for his help. One asked for a south wind, the other for an easterly wind, both had their good reasons. Now God has to decide. You know that one of them will not get his prayers answered but God in his wisdom knows everyone's needs and if he cannot answer your prayers he will support you in your suffering.

Mahatma Gandi said he could do without food for many days, but could not do without prayer for one.

### God Answers Prayer.

*I know not by what method rare,*
*But this I know – God answers prayer,*
*I know he gives his pledged word,*
*Which tells me prayers are always heard,*
*And will be answered soon or late,*
*Though often it is hard to wait.*
*I know not if the blessing sought,*
*Will come in just the way I thought.*
*I leave my prayer with him alone,*
*Whose will is wiser than my own,*
*Assured that he will grant my quest,*
*Or send an answer far more blessed.*

(Author unknown)

# Silence is golden

Silence is golden and is a way we can sometimes save ourselves from a humiliating situation.

Silence commits you to nothing.

If someone is upsetting you unjustly you can keep silent – you will put up a show of strength. Others may say: "I do not know how you managed not to blow your top."

When two people are angry they try to wound each other by words tossed to and fro like a tennis ball on the tennis court. Remember it takes two to play the game. So if one refuses to play, the game is finished.

We are weakened by what we give out and strengthened by what we hold back. Self control is an asset, so 'keep your head when all around are losing theirs'.

# God's Garden

I am sitting looking out of my window into my garden which I have named my memory garden. Many of the shrubs and plants were given to me by friends and family. Some of them are now in the spirit world but I know that I shall not forget them. As I look at these plants I remember who gave them to me.

So now let's assume that we are all seeds and that God, the divine gardener, has planted each and every one of us in this garden of life.

The gardener takes his seeds, he plants them in the dark earth, feeds and waters them and waits patiently for the seeds to push their way through; to see the stems unfurl, the leaves unfold, and the buds blossom into flower. So the divine gardener plants every one of his children in circumstances where he knows that they can flourish and grow the best.

When we plant our seeds we cannot expect the plants to be all alike. Each one will be different, this will be caused by many things. Some will be attacked by insects and disease and this will spoil the beauty of the bloom. It is the same in the garden of life, through sickness and accidents we see the blooms suffer and they do not bloom and grow as the divine gardener intended, although the seeds may come from the same source.

We plant our seeds, we keep them warm and, if you're like me, you talk to them and protect them. When the seedlings are ready to be planted out, the gardener will have prepared and cultivated the ground where they will grow and bloom. He knows some plants do not like the sun and have to be protected from it; some plants need dry soil; others need wet soil. They all have different needs, so we like the seedlings, in early life, are protected and cultivated by our parents until we are ready to be planted out into the garden of life and grow on our own roots.

There are many kinds of flowers that make up the garden, large and small ones, colours a-plenty, and the gardener places each flower where it will give the best effect. He places the colours that blend together and it's the same in this garden of life. Over the years God has gradually transplanted his people so they are now mixed together but you know that in this garden of life we do not blend together like the flowers as the divine gardener planned. Many times our 'colours' (of temperament) do not blend with those around us and you have heard it said that we have shown our 'true colours'. When we look at the outside covering, we must remember it is from within that the plant comes and when looking at someone we must not forget that the true self is within.

An incident from my working days comes to mind. I remember a young man who was a grumbler – nothing ever seemed right for him. One day he was given a task to do. As usual he complained: "I need special tools." "We will get them," said the Foreman, "Wait there. I will be ten minutes." The young man sat beside me, and we began to talk. I will never know how the subject turned to religion but it did. His tools arrived and smiling I said to him that I would never have thought that I would have had such a conversation with him. I realised my mistake when he said: "You of all people should know better because when I remove these overalls and walk out of the gate I am a different man."

So we must learn to accept those from different flower beds. The 'plants' may have been trained in a different manner, by a different language or custom or through a different religion, yet they have their roots in the same soil and they have their place in the garden of life.

At times I am sure you have felt like a rose in a bed of nettles and you know how the nettle can sting. Maybe you have been stung. But the nettle can be a friend. It can be used in herbal treatment to alleviate pain and to provide nourishment – also it makes a good beer – so we all have a purpose in life. It would be folly to try to grow into a sunflower if you were meant to be a snowdrop. We must not pretend to be something we are not. ✕

The gardener knows his plants. If the gentle life-giving rain turns into a drenching torrent and pushes them down into the ground, they do not give in, for after the rain comes the sun and they turn their faces to the warm sun and rise up strong again. If the frost puts its shrivelled fingers upon their life, they do not whither and die. They sink their roots down firmer into the warm earth. This is what we must do in the garden of life – sink our roots into faith in God and seek his warmth and his love. Just as the seed planted in the darkness of the earth, germinates, flourishes and grows ever towards the light so must we grow towards God's light.

We know that the flowers are always growing even at times when we do not see them. The spring bulb waits until it is the right time to bloom and you know that after we have suffered a long winter they bring joy to us all. We long to see the first snowdrop, for it heralds the coming of spring and you, like the snowdrop, must grow in the warm rays of the spiritual truth of a real life. We have all got the same advantage because we are all generated by one great source.

We need to look more closely at the many problems existing in the garden of life. People must get together and plant seeds of love, joy and truth. These are the flowers we want to see blooming in the garden of life. We want to find peace in our own garden and in the garden of life. It is important to be in this state of mind. This state of being is to be living true to one's purpose but sadly most people do not realise the God-potential lying with themselves. So many people cannot or will not realise that they have within their grasp an energy which has never been seen on this earth but we are allowed to tap into it now and again. Sadly so many people turn their attention to the outside world for the purpose of physical survival and entertainment but the true and real joy of life, and the real fulfilment of purpose of one's life, is not found without but rather within.

Harmony, peace and love can be created in this world by the thoughts of mankind. It is for thinking people such as yourselves, as individuals and as groups, to bring your thoughts to life and bring harmony into this world. Just like the gardener who has a great understanding of his plants, the different types and colours and their needs, we in turn must try and understand the needs of others of all types and colours. A greater effort towards friendship is needed between all individuals no matter what creed, colour, or race. True friendship is far deeper and more meaningful – it lies deep within your heart. We must realise that for true friendship to exist between two people, you must be totally honest to the real self.

The time has come for all religions, all people to unite together as one harmonious force, motivated by a desire to create peace and love in the garden of life.

* * * * *

The inspiration for 'God's Garden' was cultivated in 1984 when I was looking at a poem and card given to me by my mother. Since then I have shared it with seventy church congregations.

The card depicted a flower. In the centre was little see-through plastic container; inside it was a mustard seed. She had told me that when we were small, my sisters and I, they were a little short of money and this card had been sent to her by her brother with a ten shilling note in it – a large sum in those days. She said, 'God answers prayers and his provision is in all things.'

I still have the card with the seed intact. It is more than a hundred years old. The verse in the card reads –

*With this little mustard seed*
*there comes a special prayer,*
*that God will bless you always*
*and keep you in his care.*

There was no author's name on the following poem and she may have composed it herself, as she did sometimes.

### The Re-Awakening

The smallest hint of joys to come,
Makes a sad heart sing.
The smallest bud upon a tree,
A swallow on the wing,
The first bright hint of sunlight gold
That seems so far away
Heart's warming moments,
When no one could feel dismayed.

The earth may still look bare and cold
But when the first snowdrop peeps
We know that nature never dies,
But only falls asleep.
Eternal life, eternal hopes,
Forever shall remain,
So long as the turning of the year
Brings springtime's joy again.

My wife, Joyce often joins me in singing this song:

If I should plant a tiny seed of love
In the garden of your heart,
Would you let it grow to be a great
Big love one day,
Or would it die and fade away,
Would you care for it
And tend it every day,
Until the day when we must part,
If I should plant a tiny seed of love,
In the garden of your heart.

# Independent
# or inter-dependent?

ne of the facts of life we must come to terms with is that we depend on one another. You might be thinking at this moment I am self supporting – no one gives me anything – I am totally independent.

When you sit down to breakfast, put your cornflakes in the bowl or toast under the grill, remember it was the farmer who grew the corn and the wheat. We need the miller and the baker before we can have the toast to eat. Even the grill has to have power and so it goes on .

You have probably heard it said that man cannot live by bread alone. He needs meat and fruit. The man who grows the fruit may eat very little of it himself but he needs what others have produced to survive. If you think about it, before the end of breakfast, you are in debt to about half of the world. A French man may have produced the soap you washed your face with; a Pacific islander the sponge; a Turk the towel; your linen from the Irish man; morning tea from China or India; your bacon could have come from a farm in Berkshire or from Denmark. If you have tomatoes they may have been grown in Guernsey or Spain with the oranges for the marmalade.

How can you say you are independent? The harvest festival brings our dependence home to us. Realising how much we depend upon one another. Let us note how essential it is to get along with one another. We need a far deeper and a stronger basis of understanding between all people throughout the world.

# 'There's gold in them there hills'

oday people are spoilt for choice. They have to make many decisions everyday – most of them do not require great thought or deliberation. The manner in which we make these everyday decisions builds in us the qualities that enable us to handle major problems easily. Decision making is important. We all admire a person who is decisive and confident, who can handle their affairs with surety.

We all have these qualities, for within each and everyone is a spirit of wisdom. We may think that we are lacking in wisdom but there is an innate intelligence in us that we call upon as we turn to God in prayer. When there is any need for wisdom, the intelligence of God inspires us and directs us. Take a few moments during the day to acknowledge this spirit and quietly listen to its directions and you will find that positive thoughts will offer a change in understanding of a difficult situation, maybe presenting a solution to a problem.

No sincere prayer goes unanswered. Many prayers that seem to have gone unanswered have received a different approach from God. We ask God for some blessing and sometimes it seems he does not grant us our request. This is because he, in his infinite wisdom, is able to do better for us. We ask for bodily help or relief and he sees that we are in need of a far deeper spiritual blessing. God answers the needs of our spiritual self before he responds to our material requests.

We ask for material things but he does not give them to us. Instead he bestows upon us a spiritual blessing which will enrich us forever. When we are carrying a burden we pray for help. If help is not forthcoming, he will make sure that we receive a new influx of the power of the spirit, or he allows us the privilege of a visit from the spirit world, to minister to us.

Wherever God puts us he has some definite purpose there for us to do. Every time we find ourselves in a certain situation or if an opportunity arises where we can be of service, we may well stop and ask ourselves if God has brought us to this point for this very reason.

We are always under orders but often the orders are sealed and are opened only at the hour of need. If we realise this then it gives the most ordinary life a sacredness that we are continually serving God.

Never forget that the gifts from spirit are 'pure gold' and if we were prospectors looking for gold, before we began to dig, we would have to believe that there was 'gold in them there hills'. We would then set up our apparatus and begin to dig. As we dig, water is there to wash away the dirt and hopefully we find some gold dust. As we dig deeper, we find a few small nuggets, then larger fragments and with luck the main vein.

Now Spiritualism is the hill, and we are the prospectors. First we find the gold dust. Then a nugget or two – a fragment here and there but when we obtain the treasures of the spirit, they are more priceless than pure gold because they cannot be stolen. They do not decay and the only way to lose them is to misuse or abuse them.

Ask yourself has your life changed since you became a Spiritualist? Thoughts and feelings are now of prime importance. We must overcome pride, jealousy and destructive thoughts and lead a life of helpful and kindly service to others. This is the way we create our future heaven or hell. Reject the dross. Find the gold in our Spiritualism. Believe – *know* just like the prospector – there is 'gold in them there hills'.

All I can say to you is –

> *Climb every mountain,*
> *Ford every stream,*
> *Follow every rainbow,*
> *Till you find your dream!*

# Teamwork

Champions again

Saturdays have always been a day for sport and, if you are a fan, when the season ends, it seems that our lives become devoid of something to talk about. Yes, Saturday is a day to knock, throw or kick a ball.

In life we have all experienced knocks and we seem to be thrown in every direction. I am sure we feel that we have been kicked around many times. Now, we all know about team work; if the team is going to succeed then all the players must work together towards the common goal. Every football team wants to win the F.A. cup. It's the dream of every player to lift the cup from beneath the stadium's iconic arch. But we have to remember that the road to Wembley starts months before the final match.

There are always favourites. The form book suggests this and makes them odds on to win but you know that sometimes there is an underdog who, on the day, excels and upsets the odds, despite the fact it is the poorest team. By working together and having nothing to lose, they show that teamwork wins through. They face the challenge together, turning around what had been perhaps a difficult year.

It's not just the players on a sports field who face daunting situations and challenging circumstances. We all face times when life threatens to overwhelm us – when we are uncertain – when the problems we face seem more than we can cope with. These are the times we can feel weighed down with care; the future looks bleak; no one understands or cares and we feel so alone.

The good news is that we do not have to face these problems on our own. No matter how overwhelming the odds are, or how daunting the situation, remember, your Father God will support you. The power of the spirit will help you through the tough times in your life. Do not ever be afraid to team up with God he is your best defence.

When I played football I never heard the phrase 'professional foul' but today it is accepted as normal. They say that matches can be won on the drawing board. Footballers today do not seem half as fit and prepared for the task in hand.

I know that in my spiritual life if there is any foul play, I am aware that I have broken my vows and that I will have to accept the consequences. As for planning ahead, that's ok if everything goes to plan. As my mother quoted to me many years ago – 'man can plan but God will decide'.

During my life, I have seen many changes on the sport's field. The rules have been revised, the games have been speeded up and the goal keeper has to kick the ball more. In rugby league kicking has been minimized. Where there were heavy forwards now they are fast and fit.

Cricket has also changed as well as the three-day matches, which often got bogged down, there is what is called twenty-twenty cricket. This speeds up the game as there are only twenty 'overs' to be played by each team and the team that gets the most runs wins. This means the players have to throw caution to the wind as they take more risks to win.

Twenty-twenty cricket may lack some of the old coaching manual shots on how to protect the wicket but the crowds love it. There is no room to play safety shots. Attack is the best form of defence. He who dares wins. Batsmen get one chance and a split second to pick their shot. Sometimes they have to take risks.

Away from the ground – how is your innings going? At most funerals I have attended someone says: "They have had a good innings." Sometimes in life we get caught out and find that we are on a 'sticky wicket'. The reality is that we only get one shot at life and only in this life does God offer us a chance of eternal life.

When you take the spiritualist bat you are batting to protect your whole self. The risks are slim if you follow your principles. Remember at all times that you are batting for a good place in that eternal home, in God's presence.

We have to ask ourselves whether the changes in the games have improved it. Have they made the games more exciting, or even better? Whether the rules are easier to understand and whether more people are coming to watch.

Now is the time to pick our team. What position do you desire? Do you want to be a striker or a goal scorer? They seem to be always in the forefront. You could be a defender, a centre back who controls the defence, or a midfielder who takes the ball forward and feeds the forward line – the one who has the responsibility to be up with the forwards in attack and in defence when needed.

Friends, just think – this is your life. In life we do all these things, at work, in family life or in any organization in which we serve. Now we have to remember in the game of life the back room staff who prepare everything for the big day, the groundsmen, the cleaners, the tea ladies and many more. Without them nothing would be possible. At the top comes the management and of course the main directors.

Now I will ask my manager, my Father God, for his help to improve my abilities in every position he asks me to play.

Remember, *Teamwork* is the glue that brings it all together.

# Life's mysteries

When I was walking through the city centre observing men at work cleaning a stone building these thoughts came to me.

Life is a mystery and no one can live without finding out the truth of that saying. I realise nothing in this world fits perfectly in place until the edges have been trimmed off. Our whole life is a cutting process and when we are ready to fit into our corner, wherever it be, we find there are other edges to be trimmed off before we can really fit into it.

The great secret is that it is you yourself that must be fitted to the corner and not the corner to you. Many waste their time laboriously working at their corner trying to shape it to themselves when it would take very little time, and a lot less trouble, to cut off their own edges and fit themselves into the corner.

From birth to death, life is a mystery. In fact the longer we live the more mysteries we experience. Most people will say that the greatest mystery is death but if you ask me I would say it is life, earthly life. We all know it is the school in which we experience many things. For instance how can one tell the feelings of another and who can fathom the depth of those feelings. We should deal tenderly with the feelings of others.

How would we know that sunshine and harmony were blessings unless the contrast of shadow and storm had taught us so? We feel grief and pain while on this earth. Then when the worries of life soften and we find strength, we say it's a mystery how we have found the strength to overcome it.

The objectives in life of discovery are not just outside but inwardly as well. Each day is a new experience in your life. We have likes and dislikes but to express it more strongly – we have love and hate. Then, to express it more scientifically, we have attraction and repulsion. These emotions we experience more than anything else in life.

Like – Dislike, Love – Hate, Attraction – Repulsion: you seem to be powerless when they come into your life. You dislike certain people – more than that – you are not at ease in their presence, you distrust them, you are not happy with them. You cannot give a reason why – it's a mystery. Yet on the other hand we have the law of attraction. You feel that you can trust certain people, you feel at ease with them and you are stronger and inspired and more confident by their presence.

The experience of love and hate is nearer to us and there are many who join themselves together, but only a few experience the mystery of true love.

So each day we wait for the mysteries to unfold and as we look at all these different states of life, we realise that it is impossible to keep in any state perfectly. We cannot love all the time and I'm sure we could not or should not hate forever. Things do change, for this is the way of life's mysteries. You learn more and more, day by day, of the mysteries contained in God's world.

If our inward faith burns brightly we have progressed. Our faith sometimes grows dim but it can be rekindled. The best way is by spiritual faith and not solely by material knowledge but they can and do go together. With material knowledge and spiritual faith we can see more mysteries open up. Sometimes it seems unbelievable. How many times has someone been ill and with faith, not only in the doctors and surgeons, but faith in God and the spirit healers, they have overcome an illness or disability.

What is life but the schooldays of the spirit – the learning time as it were, to fit us for a future life. How would children take their place in this busy world if they were not taught? How would their interests develop or thoughts gain experience if they were not given tasks to learn? In life your tasks are hard and varied, so many in fact, that no one teacher can prepare you and many take a hand in your development. You are taught by pain and joy by sorrow and love and many other aspects. There are many masters who have their turn in your education.

As we learn our lessons we progress but if you have wasted your opportunities whilst at school you suffer afterwards. This applies both materially and spiritually. We have to look to the future – that is something we have to wait for. Do not run to it. Stand patiently in the present until the future comes to you. Ask old people if you think the present is cruel. Remember that the cruel present could be necessary to shape you for the future.

Many live today by the old saying – 'Eat, drink and be merry, for tomorrow we die'. And die tomorrow we might. So how many of us are prepared? We do not look at a man on the outside. We find the truth about ourselves under the surface. God looks at man as a whole.

We who are Spiritualists must band together and begin to build a new life for ourselves. Clear away the old debris of the past and do not allow any of it to be used in the new future we are building for ourselves .

Let me put it this way. In many of our towns and cities scaffolding appeared and with it came the cleaners who sandblasted the buildings. Over the years many layers of soot and grime had built up over the stone work, completely obscuring any architectural beauty. For years no one had noticed the building. Weeks later, the building had been transformed – it gleamed. People stood back to admire the design and the craftsmanship of the old building which had not been seen for so long because of the dirt. Now the lovely building stood out.

We can compare the building to ourselves. By giving ourselves a new look, others will stand back and admire us and want to follow, for people are looking for a new way of life. In some ways we are like old buildings, we have to undergo some form of restoration. When you feel down and life seems to be giving you a raw deal ask God in your prayers to enfold you in his spirit, where peace, love and harmony reigns supreme.

If you are looking at Spiritualism for a new way of life, I can say that Spiritualism is real and of great worth.

Many have given it a thought and sparingly inquired into its truth. Much has been written by those who claim it is unchristian. They cannot justify their views.

Much can be obtained in your search for evidence of the reality of the unseen world and a future life.

Other religions are eager to condemn and say it's fraud. Well let them take heed. Those who belittle this great truth – to the scoffers it is denied, but the genuine seeker into its truth will find treasures beyond compare. Seek in earnest; approach with respect its demands and obey the one eternal law – to love and help each other.

> *It is far better to lead your life as if*
> *there is a God, when perhaps there isn't,*
> *than to lead it as if there isn't,*
> *and then find there is.*
>
> *Goethe*

# Fruits of the spirit

It is said that if one were standing on a thick rubber mat, one could touch a live wire without harm, because electricity will not come in unless it can go out. The same is true of the power of the spirit. We must not want the power of the spirit for ourselves but to share it with others. Remember the power will come in when it can get out so it may be used for the benefit of mankind.

Again we must remember that so many of the gifts of God can only be used by those who undergo the disciplining of one's self. Without this discipline the gifts are valueless. Think of the words of the hymn that we sing – *Come, Holy Spirit, come*, but do we as healers and mediums understand that this power of the spirit is holy.

Spiritual contact is not just the relaying of messages, because each and everyone can be a message bearer by sending out thoughts of love and trying to understand others. Always someone needs sympathy and every one of us can drop seeds of kindness.

I recently read a story where a man dreamt he entered a place in which the gifts of God were kept. Behind the counter stood the store keeper. In his dream the would-be purchaser said: "I have run out of the fruits of the spirit, can you re-stock me?"

He thought he would be refused and so he shouted loudly: "In place of war, injustice, lying and hate I want peace, justice, truth, love and joy. Without these I shall be lost."

The store man replied: "We do not stock the fruits of the spirit. We keep only the seed. A lot of hard work has to be put in before you can reap the fruits of your sowing."

\* \* \* \* \*

*The episode of earth life is a force
of great value,
In developing character,
In enlarging knowledge,
In cultivating new friendships
And generally adding to the richness of life.*

# The changing scenes of life

This morning I visited my sister and her husband. They are Salvationists; both have played in the band for many years but now the years have caught up with them. They need all their breath to get around but they have their memories on tapes. They listen to themselves playing. As I entered I was greeted with the tune – *Through all the changing scenes of life.*

I suppose people of my age could say that we have seen more changes than any other generation. Change is something we cannot avoid. Many times we do not agree but we have to accept the changes and adapt.

We cannot expect that things will always remain the same but amid the changing conditions and circumstances in our world, and in our individual lives and affairs, we can be assured of a changeless source of light and understanding.

The unchanging wisdom of God is always with us to reveal right ways. Truth is unchanging. Hold fast to your truth and do not fear other changes or resist them. If we flow along with the good, we will grow along with the good.

# Seasons

et us feel the gladness of spring, which pulses through all the earth at the coming of new life. Let us feel the glory of summer, when all of life is in full bloom. Like the earth, whose children we are, we shall find no sadness in the winds of autumn and the falling leaves. They foretell the winter; not a death, but a time of sleep from which we shall reawaken to the glory of spring.

As I gaze from my window, changes are taking place. I can see primroses in bloom and the magpies collecting twigs for their nest. This tells us that new life is soon to follow. Even in the smallest garden the rhythm of the seasons can not only be seen but heard. Though the flowers and plants go noiselessly through their processes of germination, maturity and winter sleep, the rhythm is not a silent one but simply unheard or unnoticed by many who work or sit in the garden. It is a constant accompaniment of movement and sound of life, never-ending.

If you feel that your burdens are insurmountable, look at the cold, hard pavement and see the spring grass flourishing against all attempts to crush it out of existence. Take courage and meditate on this short verse:

> If in your store, two loaves alone are left,
> Sell one and with the dole,
> Buy Hyacinths to feed the soul.

As I write, it is the first day of spring. In the springtime all around us is new life. Nature sings her song of a new beginning. I have just been for a walk around the garden. The violets have returned in all their loveliness. I have removed the dandelions from the lawn because they too have returned with all their persistence. Everywhere there is new life springing forth.

Sometimes in our lives we need springtime or a time when we can begin again. If we are at such a 'time' and 'place' in life, let us prepare for new growth and the change we want to see, feel and experience. Our lives can be filled with new colour and beauty. The persistence of the dandelion teaches us never to give up or give in and that we can trust in the blossoming of the God-potential within us. Let us bless every sign of new growth in our lives, in our thoughts and emotions, as well as in this lovely world around us and let us thank God for the power to begin again.

Now, as we move into the summertime, the hymn written by W. W. How tells us that – *Summer suns are glowing over land and sea*. Summer is here. The seed of all life lies in the dark until it is time to waken and then, after the trials and tribulations of the growing pains of experience, it comes to life. We all have our discouraging times when things don't go well for us, when everything seems to go wrong. How could it be otherwise? For, if we could go through life easily, what would be the point?

The storms and dark clouds which are life's winter can only be pointers to the brighter and happier days of summer. Should your path of life now be clouded with pain and unhappiness, realise that we grow under the apparent darkness of what we consider to be our disadvantages. Do not despair, for these may turn out to be our most indispensable advantages.

We all have hidden, undeveloped characters. We all have powers which we have barely begun to exercise. Everyone at some time or another begins to question the purpose of life. Some come into our churches and there we can teach them that, by being patient, and developing the inner self (the true self), pointers to the future are given. We often find that the circumstances of life have either set us on a course we have to travel with difficulty or, by some unknown chance, we have been guided on to a desired path which our inspirers intended us to walk.

Some schools of thought say that our destinies are planned out for us and that whether we like it or not, we shall automatically go the way allotted to us. Others, equally convinced, say that man is a free agent and the master of his own fate – so we have a divergence of opinions.

Truth, like a diamond, has many facets and can be viewed from many angles, so no man can say he possesses the whole truth. The final truth is beyond the understanding of all human beings but, as the seasons change, summer allows us to see that there is as much beauty in a tiny flower as there is in a majestic tree, or in the smallest gem, as in the highest mountain.

When I was a school boy everyone looked forward to the summer holidays. The school and factories and the coal mines closed down for two weeks and the lucky ones were those who could afford a week at the coast. Today we have more holiday time and today people travel to far-away places and arrive home to tell us of the wonderful sights they have seen.

Travellers to Norway describe how they have stood amongst the mighty peaks, awed by their grandeur. Those who visit Italy have walked on the ruined streets of ancient cities. Whilst travelling, people may make a visit to a church. When in Rome it's a must to visit the Vatican City and wherever people go on holiday, at home or abroad, they often find themselves in a church. Most of us would not find time to visit our own city's art galleries or museums and yet, on holiday, we find time to take a look.

A walk in the park? Don't feel like it today! But on holiday, how many of us would do so? A good number, I would say.

People today see more of earth's beautiful and wonderful things than in the past. Travellers through Egypt look at the Pyramids' large stones and cannot imagine how, all those years ago, in what was considered a primitive world, it was possible to transport the stones into the middle of the desert and then lift them to the great heights. The hymn tells us:

> *The world has much that's beautiful,*
> *If man could only see.*

We must not miss an opportunity to look at beautiful things.

As autumn moves in with the changing the colours of the leaves on the trees, it is time for the farmers to reap what they have sown. Autumn to me is pay-back time. This year I have watched the gladioli at the bottom of my garden. These I planted to cover the fence but with each passing year they have degenerated and this year they are not very good at all. In fact a good gardener would have uprooted them long ago. They are long and scraggy. The leaves look very anaemic and they should be dead – in fact one or two are.

However, others have fought their way through four winters, survived the cold winds and snow and struggled to produce another, if rather pathetic, show. They don't seem so bad, if we take into account the struggle they have had to produce their blooms. I have not helped, for I have not played my part in assisting them over the years so, I have to admit, they have done their best under poor circumstances.

Life for some people may be hard in one way or another. You could say that they have not had a real chance, that everything seems to be against them and yet, like the gladioli, they have struggled through, surviving all the odds. What amazes me is not that people are so brave but that, things being as they are, they are so good. As I look at the condition of people across the world, at the wickedness and ugliness, I realise we must help, for if we don't then they will be like my gladioli in a very short time.

I was looking at the pansies too, their little faces looking up at me – they are beautiful. I remember my mother saying that the spelling of the name 'Pansies' gives us – Patience, Attentiveness, Neatness, Sincerity, Industry, Earnestness and Self- Sacrifice. This gave me a new respect for the humble flower.

My friend says that winter is the hardest season. It is cold, frosty and dull, and nothing happens. Everything is tired and ready to hibernate. Many people who live in countries that have cold winters travel abroad seeking the warm sun. I suppose that as we travel through our lives we all experience the seasons and every common walk of life is worthwhile if you could see the beauty of God's work.

My favourite poem is *The Daffodils* by Wordsworth. The daffodils he wrote about grew beside Ullswater in the Lake District but in fact he saw them time and time again in his memory. He would lie down to relax and he tells us:

> *They flash upon that inward eye*
> *Which is the bliss of solitude.*

I think this is a wonderful description of the memory.

We are all making memories in our 'todays' as we prepare for our 'tomorrows' so that when we reach the wintertime of life, we can look back and thank God for bringing us through the sunshine and shadows of the past. You may think that you have laboured in vain and have accomplished nothing. Your lives may seem to have become dormant but remember, every step you take is towards better things. There is nothing to fear in the future. Every experience, whether of joy or sorrow, will help you. In every disaster you will find goodness 'in folds', as they say.

So, as the russet-gold of late autumn is gently and imperceptibly refined into the silver of winter, we withdraw into our homes early to find our cosy spot and shut out the winter cold. Then, as a new year approaches, people reflect back on the past and judge the effect it has left on their lives.

For some it may have been a year of happiness and prosperity. Others will tell you they will be glad to see the old year out – a year that has been difficult – a year that it would be nice if they could just put that part behind them and start anew. But remember your labours are not in vain. Your life may seem, with all its activities, to be getting poor results but they reach back into the unseen – and who knows what blessings they become or what impressions they leave on other lives now and on into eternity. Just as, when each year ends, wintertime carries on into the New Year, when life on earth is over we will be born again in the springtime of eternal life in the spirit world.

The memory is a precious gift. It allows us to go back in time and cheer ourselves by reliving the happiest moments in our lives, and you don't have to be special to see lovely things in the mind's eye. I think this poem I found finishes this journey through the seasons perfectly. The author is unknown.

*The Memory*

*Funny thing is the memory, a conjurer, I'd say*
*Or so it seems as I look back*
*to things of yesterday*

*For half the sorrows are forgot and I remember best*
*The sunshine lighting up my road,*
*the times when I've been blessed*

*The ill are lost, the good remain and the worst is*
*left behind*
*And all life's precious little joys*
*Have nested in my mind.*

# Picking up the pieces

o you remember the song from the Fred Astaire film – *Pick yourself up, Dust yourself off*?

This was brought to my mind a few days ago when I dropped a dish while washing-up – not that I'm chained to the kitchen sink! As I picked up the pieces, I asked: "Where did we get it from?" As it was part of a set, we looked back and remembered who had given it to us and why. Looking at what was once a beautiful dish now in small pieces, I wished that I could have stuck it together again but I knew that was impossible. I had to take care as I picked up each piece and I started to think, that when we have a broken relationship, of whatever kind, we have to take care not to make things worse as we pick up the pieces.

I suppose I could have walked away, and let someone else pick up the pieces – that would have been easy to do. But then someone else may have got hurt whilst doing something for which they had not been responsible.

The reasons for the failure of a relationship are many and varied. Although they sometimes may seem very trivial, exaggerated and out of all proportion, pride stands in the way and we say: "It's not my fault, why should I make the first move?" However, we must to realise that if someone does not make that first move to put things right, no matter how hurt or offended they may feel, waiting will make it harder to pick up the pieces.

Making the first move should not be looked upon as a weakness, but as a strength to overcome self and to show to others the spiritual side of our nature. Many times in my life I have been tempted to walk away from the things that I believed in most – but I stopped and looked at the situation, picked up the pieces and walked tall. We have to try our very best to show to others that we have overcome the trial.

They say that when things go wrong in your life, seek out your friends. In many instances, that is the time when you find who your true friends are. When a relationship or a friendship comes to an end it is usually because someone has been deceitful. You will find that deception is difficult to deal with, especially when you are deceived by someone you love.

I suppose the next question is – can things be put right? In most cases I would say yes. There is no better way to begin again than to say, 'I'm sorry'. I know that sometimes it is very hard to bring oneself to say these two little words if it is you who is in the wrong.

Be up front and honest, ready to be humble and try to learn a lesson from your mistakes.

Picking up the pieces is not an easy task. Trying to piece things together takes time and just when you think you have got all the pieces together again, something happens and you have to start all over again to rebuild. I dare say I could have picked up all the broken bits of the dish and stuck them together again. I know that I would have had to use a strong substance to make a strong bond. Also, it would have taken time and patience.

When we start to rebuild our relationships or friendships we need clear out all the old debris and start anew with a foundation of love. No matter how big a mess you have made of life you can begin again. The new pattern will not be quite like the old one. Yet, we might find it satisfying and we may be able to grow from our experience.

As the song says –

*Nothing's impossible I have found,*
*For when my chin is on the ground,*
*I pick myself up,*
*Dust myself off,*
*Start all over again.*

# What's in a word?

**eculiar**

I remember when I told my mother that I was going to the Spiritualist church, she said that people would think that I was peculiar. So I decided to look up the word in the dictionary.

I found that the word 'peculiar' is a word with several meanings.

It can mean 'Odd', 'Strange', 'Different' but it can also mean 'Special',

'Exceptional',

'Particular'   or –

'Appropriate'.

When there is a good cause crying out for support or a wrong to be righted, all too often the people who give their support are labeled – peculiar.

Many people are afraid of being thought peculiar, when electing to do individual things, or speaking their minds freely. But what is at first thought 'peculiar' becomes the norm, if just a few have the courage to support those who give the lead.

# 'Bob the Builder'

*ob the builder, can he fix it?* asks the song from
the children's series. The song insists that
whatever the problem – *Fix it, Bob can.*

With the threat of global warming, huge injustices,
famine, war, disease and death all around, we may
indeed ask whether God, the builder can fix his broken
world.

In the past people in this world blamed God for
everything and if something bad happened – it was
God's will; declaring that God was punishing them for
their wickedness and it was for their own good –
anything good, of course was a reward.

One of the most important things in the world is
that we should have a true sense of values, and in spite
of all the hostile forces that threaten to destroy it or
undermine it, we should be striving to repair and
maintain it.

What do we mean by a sense of values?

We mean our assessment of those things which are
of great worth.

I wonder if – just by chance – we could take this old
world to an Antiques Roadshow what the dealer would

say. Probably that it was corroded in parts and had wear and tear in the ozone layers; that most of its wealth had been extracted from it and there was need for restoration... . There is an old saying that the best things in life are free but through man's greed the countryside is slowly disappearing. Modern life has made it increasingly difficult for us to keep our sense of values. Most people in the world are too busy chasing wealth, fame and indulging themselves in the many pleasures this world has on offer, without a thought of God.

If there is a weak link in this chain of thought I cannot find it and the whole chain seems to indicate the moral running through the whole story of life. The moral story is co-operate with God for he is working out a purpose that is greater and grander than any human mind can grasp. We have to remember that a sense of values is not something you can switch on and off like a television.

At this moment two words come to mind – 'Thank God!' I'm sure at sometime in your life you have spoken these two words.

I remember as a child going on holiday to Norfolk, staying with an aunt and uncle on their farm. We always spent our summer holidays in Norfolk, my mother's birth place. She came from a large farming family.

I remember one year, after the harvest had been gathered in, my uncle said that on Sunday he was going to chapel, of course we all accompanied him. On the way we met another uncle, also a farmer, who asked: "Where are you going?"

"To chapel," his brother said: "to thank God for a good harvest that he has provided."

The reply came: "But I ploughed the field and planted the corn."

The answer came back: "Don't you forget you were guided by the spirit."

I'm sure there is some truth in that and that it needs team-work in all things, whatever the circumstances, and that God's provision in all things is bountiful and perfect.

I have learned from experience to overcome life's difficulties by placing my trust in the Great Spirit. The secret lies in accepting the situation. I hope you realise the future is in your hands – not only your personal future but this poor old world's.

Remember everything we do affects someone else. We can as Spiritualists send out healing thoughts to the world and help to heal it. For yourself, every day is full of the realisation of the power of God within you wanting to help. The power of the Great Spirit is all around, no matter where you are. The power moves through you to touch everyone you come into contact with.

You can become a channel for the spirit to work with. You are in contact with everything around you, because you are all one with each other, as the waves are all one with the ocean. The aim is to help us realise a little more truly how great God is.

And then to get across all the revelations of God, we must practise our religion at all times. We must show the world that Spiritualism is vast and of great value. Remember our pioneers paid a huge price for it. We have been told and have read many times how our pioneers met and challenged all the oppression that faced them, even defying the law. Now that responsibility has been handed down to us.

We are the caretakers who have to preserve and keep the brightness of Spiritualism glowing for others.

The purpose of life is to build a character that is fitted by what we have learned in earth's school. No other can live your life for you and nobody can carry the weight, nor take it from your shoulders. You are responsible for all you say, do or think – here and in the hereafter.

To conclude, Spiritualism is a revelation. It is a source of teaching which lifts man to a higher understanding of truth, which carries with it all the responsibilities of a religion inspired by the spirit. The question now is what are we looking for in our spiritual life? Have we got our sense of values right and remember – the good things in life do not come cheap.

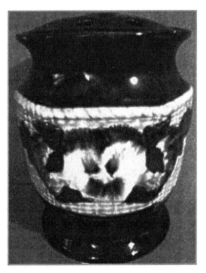

*One of my special things*

# Courage

A friend of mine was diagnosed as terminally ill and given a short time to live. Unless we ourselves are placed in that same position I am sure we could not perceive the devastation which takes place, at all levels, in the life of someone who has just been told that they have a short number of weeks to live.

My friend came to terms with the situation, putting his affairs in order and making the best of life.

One day he decided to visit his sister, who lived some miles away. Whilst there he became ill; his sister called an ambulance; he was admitted to hospital and underwent an operation – one which his own local hospital had decided was impossible to perform – that was some ten years ago.

He is not cured. He is still under medication, but what a change this experience has made to his life.

With determination he has accomplished many things. He has become a good artist, producing portraits; made beautiful table lamps with coloured glass; welding wrought iron; making garden furniture and gates. He has mastered the computer and gone 'on-line'; bought a boat; sailed on the waterways and likes to include a little fishing.

He has made many new friends; taken trips abroad; living life to the full; taking each day as it comes; keeping busy. His new passion is the digital camera taking pictures of all the beautiful things that he has made and the sunrise and sunsets along the waterways.

So sometimes sorrow and suffering bring new challenges and opportunities – a disappointment can change your outlook on life. Many who have been made redundant feel lost and useless but out of the unhappiness new pathways are made; other avenues are pursued; a new life is built and happiness rekindled as they find a new rock on which to rebuild their lives.

I believe in the power of prayer and, having been on the receiving end many times, more than once, I have found myself lifted up and carried over the critical point. It may well be that the prayers of unknown people in far-away places were helping me in ways I could not know. We understand very little about the power of prayer and it is possible to misuse it even with the highest motives.

I think we can only ask that God's will be done in regards to any situation. People in need seek him and know his love and truth directly but by the very act of asking – if it is done sincerely and without reserve – we open ourselves as channels for God's healing power.

The power of prayer linked with the power of positive thinking can be a substantial help in your life – believe in yourself, have faith in your abilities. Too many people are defeated by everyday problems of life.

How many of us can place our hands on our hearts and say in all honesty, that our life has been changed – very few. It is not so much the troubles and tragedies that mar our happiness and contentment, it is the breakdown in the harmony of our day-to-day existence; something wrong with the daily round that most seriously interferes with the joy in living which should be our birthright.

The troubles, tragedies and the worries in life, if only because of the urgency and drama, call forth our reserve and we often meet them half-way. Remember, it is not the great splashes of water that wear away the stones but the steady falling of the smallest drops, and so it is with us, our resistance is broken by the relentless pressure of every day friction.

How to discover, understand and overcome them is the secret of the art of happy living. Let us remember that without trial there would be no triumphs; without danger there would be no victories. Therefore we should face life squarely, conscious of its problems. We realise that every individual contains within him or her self the power to conquer every disease and master every difficulty. Everyone possesses a reservoir of strength from which they can draw in moments of need.

The kingdom of heaven is within – how little that is understood. Life consists not only of the things that you do but also of the things you say and think. Do not imagine that only your deeds count – they do to a large extent – but your words and your thoughts are also part of you. The way you contact the higher self is by living one's life in accordance with the laws of the Great Spirit.

We ought to learn well the values of opportunities, for they only come now and again. If we linger they are gone and very rarely return. I am sure, like me, you look back and say – if only I had done this or that my life would have been different.

Do not idle away your time. The song says – *time goes by so slowly* – for the young ones so it may seem, but when you have passed the three score years and ten, time flies by and sometimes your heath and weakness of the body does not allow you to fulfil your dreams – so *do it now!* Prove to yourself that you can achieve the things that will satisfy you. Then you can look back and say – *I did it my way.*

To conclude, Denis Waitley author of *Empires of the Mind* writes on how to succeed in your life. He had worked his way up from a basic upbringing, to be a successful owner of several corporations in the U.S.A. He went into all the major universities and business colleges to lecture to the students on how to become successful.

Once he was asked to join the evangelist Billy Graham to lecture in one of the largest universities in the U.S.A. Afterwards he was seated next to him at dinner, where he asked Denis Waitley: "How many lives do you think you have changed today?" After a moment of thought he replied: "Well at least one – my own but I hope what I have said will help others to self-achieve like myself."

So I hope what you have read will help you to bring about a change in your life.

A poem that was given to me seems appropriate for this story.

## Dreams

I've dreamed many dreams, that never came true,
I've seen them vanish at dawn,
But I've realised enough of my dreams, thank God,
To make me want to dream on.

I've prayed many prayers, when no answers came,
Though I waited patient and long,
But answers have come to enough of my prayers,
To make me keep praying on.

I've trusted many a friend that failed
And left me to weep alone,
But I've found enough of my friends true blue,
To make me keep trusting on.

I've sown many seeds that fell by the way
For the birds to feed upon,
But I've held enough golden sheaves in my hand,
To make me keep sowing on.

I've drained the cup of disappointment, and pain
And gone many days without song,
But I've sipped enough nectar from the roses of life,
To make me want to live on.

Ron DeMarco & Friend (© 1990)

# Day-dreams

I am sure like me, you have had day-dreams. They provide an escape from reality when we are feeling low and flights of fancy are an escape from the sometimes harsh realities of life.

We all dream of winning a windfall and what we would do. Many say nothing would change – that they would keep on working.

If only we could wave a magic wand to make our life better. However we can do better than just crossing our fingers or touching wood when lady luck seems to have abandoned us and our dreams do not seem to work out in the way we hoped. This can cause us to think there is nothing we can do to improve our life. We think that we will have to be content with our lot and to dream of anything better and more fulfilling is a waste of time. Remember the old saying – 'God helps those who help themselves'.

God will always give comfort if you ask in prayer. When you talk to him and follow his advice, you can know his peace. God's plan may cause us to reassess our priorities, aims and attitudes, but he will never desert us whatever problems we are struggling with – however long it lasts.

In life it maybe hard to find someone whom you can totally rely on. People often let you down and hurt you, even family and friends whom you thought you could trust and you find that it becomes increasingly difficult to trust anyone again. We feel let down, isolated and vulnerable but life does not have to be like this – do not let your heart be troubled. Trust in God – millions of people have and have never been let down. He can be relied on in any situation and at any-time.

When dreams do not work out the way you had hoped, maybe we should think of others and take the focus off ourselves and instead help our fellow man.

There is a story of an American poet who struggled for years to attract interest in his work. Times were tough and he was on the brink of failure when he received a letter from the great Ralph Waldo Emerson congratulating him on his work. This changed his outlook on life. So remember, a word in the right place at the right time, could alter someone's life. Encouragement is one of the central themes that overcomes disappointment and fear. Encouragement by itself does not overcome or solve a problem but it enables us to deal with it.

As you go through life you discover there are many ways to gain wisdom such as writing down and reflecting on what you have learnt through experience gleaned from the collective knowledge of others. Many people in the wider world have tried to follow their dreams; some succeed, others experience sleepless nights of worry and stress. The results of their efforts can turn out to be anything but dream-like. As the song says – *I beg your pardon, I never promised you a rose garden!* Life is not a bed of roses but if we work hard we can make life's garden something special and a place where others like to be.

I still dream about my country cottage. I watch the programmes on TV about houses. They say it's all about 'location' but I do realise that once you have moved to your dream house or whatever, it will still be just bricks and mortar and we will still have all the pressures and responsibilities of modern life.

What we should be looking for is a life-changing mission. Have you discovered one yet? As a person of more than three score years and ten, let me give you some advice – there is nothing good about getting old. Time has a way of catching you unawares. It seems like yesterday that I was young. I live near the local football field and I remembered the many times I sunk my studs into the turf. Where did all those years go? I know that I have lived them all, and I have travelled back in dream-time and remembered what it was like then.

My friends have retired and, like me, snow has covered their roof. I remember when I was young and now we are the 'old folk' that we never thought we would become. My wife says that we are in the winter-time of our lives – all that I can hope for is that we have a very long winter!

If you are not there yet, let me remind you – it will be by your side sooner than you think, so if you have any ambitions or something you want to accomplish, *do not* put it off because you can never be sure that you will see the winter out.

Remember you have no guarantee that you will complete all the seasons of your life.

Worrying about death?
Once it happens –
you can forget about it.

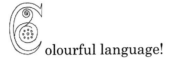olourful language!

It is said that a bird in the hand is worth two in a bush – meaning we should be satisfied with what we have, instead of risking it to get more.
Then I suppose when you have
    feathered your nest and feel that you are
      as free as a bird,
        you will need to have eagle eyes
          to keep a watch on all around you;
        for someone may be
      watching you like a hawk,
        ready to cook your goose,
          or make you a lame duck.
By now you will probably have become a night owl.
    A wise old owl will tell you to –
      always take a bird's eye view.
Fly as the crow flies
    and remember –
      one swallow does not a summer make.
But you can be sure
    that birds of a feather do flock together.

# Power of thought

I read once in a gardening magazine about the cacti. Cacti thrive in the desert, one here, another there. Each on the surface separated from the other, as if not wanting to associate with one another. But if you dig into the ground you will discover that each is linked with the other by its unseen roots.

Like the cactus each of us is an individual, each different, a distinct character in ourselves – that's how it should be – yet all of us are linked by hidden ties and purposes, and the great art of living is how to remain an individual and yet be one of a group.

It is in such deep things as love and service which bind us together. It is more than forty years ago since Joyce and I linked together, to work for spirit and I must include here short piece she wrote in 1988 for the Healing Newsletter:

### The Power of Thought.

The power of thought is a very important part of life and goes back a long way when man lived in a primitive world. It is known that thoughts could be used to kill long before they were used for the betterment of mankind. So we must cultivate our thoughts for the good of others and influence our own organism towards health and success.

Auto-suggestion is a powerful mental stimulant and can have a great effect upon mind and body, introducing positive ideas into a patient's mind concerned with well-being, suggesting the use of visualisation – seeing one's self fit and healthy; putting the thought into the patient's conscious mind which in turn will be absorbed into the subconscious.

There is a value in suggesting a form of repetitive affirmation such as – 'I am getting better and better in every way'. Also by talking to the bodily intelligence, the healer should direct his thoughts to the patient's spirit-self attempting to instill optimism and hope. 'As a man thinketh so he is.'

S.J.P   D.S.N.U.

# What a wonderful world

feel privileged to have been born at a time when so much seems to have happened. I have seen the telephone come into most peoples' homes; the wash tub exchanged for a washing machine. We have vacuum cleaners instead of carpet sweepers and the radio. As a boy, on Saturday afternoons we met at the home of one of the villagers to watch television. This then new invention was wonderful. Since then we have calculators, computers, fax machines and now the internet.

Oh! I forgot man has also walked on the moon. We have jet planes that travel faster than sound and most people own a motor car.

I have just answered a knock on the door. The little boy from next door, wants to know, do I want a pizza – just pretend he says. I have given him my order, and away he went on his tricycle, two minutes later he returned with my pretend pizza. He pretended to take my money and gave me my pretend change.

I remember when boys played engines and engine drivers but things change. The phrase 'when I win the pools' has now changed to 'when I win the lottery'. And we expect everything in an instant – instant Coffee, instant custard and meals heated in the micro-wave oven. We are continually devising and making new 'improved' products to make things faster and to perform better. We live in a push-button existence.

I suppose it's true to say that with all these new inventions, we should have time on our hands but I hear people say they have no time to spare. Whose fault is that? We should take control of our lives. These new things, good as they may be, need some of our time; the TV. controls us, the car needs our attention, there are newspapers to read and the telephone always rings when you are giving your time to something else.

I suppose people today are busier than ever before, as there are more things competing for our time and energy. To keep abreast of time is an insuperable task for most of us. Life surely does not consist of doing more things faster and in less time. Must we not ask ourselves what is the final end of all this?

I suppose we shall go so fast we shall meet ourselves coming back and end up in a whirlwind!

I must go now – my little friend is back.

Can I mend his puncture? – So some things do remain the same!

# Reflections

Arriving in hospital to have a heart by-pass I was not feeling at all well. My wife, Joyce was with me to see me settled in. I was visited by all the surgeons who would be taking part in my operation. The first one examined me. The next one looked at my legs. He was looking at the veins, selecting which leg had the best vein to use. Then came the surgeon who was going to perform the operation.

He explained the many things that could go wrong, even the possibility of death, but he assured me it was very rare. Now came the nurses who would be with me all the way. Blood had now been taken and I was taken to a private room. Visiting time ended and I said a special goodnight to my loved ones.

Then I was on my own with only my thoughts. It felt as if this was my last night on earth. My mind reflected back and I thought of all the good and bad things that had happened in my life.

Feeling very lonely in this room on my own, I closed my eyes and sent out a prayer: "Please give me someone to talk to." Little did I know that my wife, Joyce was doing the same thing. No sooner had the thought been sent out and a nurse appeared and asked if I would do them a favour by going into another ward, because there was a family whose father was very ill and needed to be private.

I agreed and found myself sharing with a man who was recovering from the operation that I was going to have. He told me what would happen and how he felt afterwards. Settling down for the night, I thought, I hope that I will be as well as my new-found friend.

I sent out my thoughts in prayer and immediately I heard the words of the hymn – *New every morning is the love* and this told me that God had answered my prayer. After my operation I looked at the hymn, this was the outcome.

*New every morning is the love,*
*Our waking and uprising prove,*
*Through sleep and darkness safely brought,*
*Restored to life and power and thought.*

This verse assures us that, just as we go to sleep at night and wake up to another day, so as we leave this world at death, we know we will wake up and be reborn in another place – heaven, paradise, the summer land – call it what you want and you will realise that you are still alive and able to think. Our thoughts maybe are the only things that go with us into the next stage of our life. It explained to me that no matter where I woke up here or in the spirit world I would be still alive.

The second verse tells to us that if our lives on earth have not been as good we would wish there is the possibility of having 'new thoughts of God' and that eternal progress is open to everyone who wants to shake off their past and rise in everlasting days.

The third verse reminds us that everything we do or say should be done with the best of intentions and with love; to love one another; to show compassion to those less fortunate than ourselves; to make peace and not war. The next verse simply says, that the common tasks in life will give us all we need and at all times try to live as near to God as possible.

We all know that this world is in need of a spiritual revival, so we must all join together in prayer for this world and that everyone will see the error of their ways; to stop plundering and abusing its riches. It is our duty to build a future for those who follow us.


I remember waking up and asking my wife, Joyce: "When do I go for my operation?" She said: "You went yesterday." – What a wonderful feeling!

Then I was told that I would be like a new man. I felt I had found the fountain of youth. I was told to walk and exercise keep fit, because what people call old age is stiffness caused by lack of physical exercise.

I realised there are other things needed, a wise combination of diet and vital foods, with regular helpings of spiritual food, thinking positive, eliminating the habits of the past.

A new man and now I have to have a new attitude towards living. I had to have an ultra-sound test they let me listen to the blood flowing through my arteries. The blood stream she told me carries cleansing new life. Every time we breathe we take in oxygen, so that it can renew the cells. I read that we inhale eighteen times a minute that's 1080 breaths an hour. Then in a day we work at renewing our body 25,000 times, so I ask you – How in the world do we grow old?

The life that God gives us is immortal. Our life force which we call human is God in expression. Moment by moment, breath by breath, by virtue of divine life, it is up to each and everyone if they want to live in the past. Through the power of the spirit we call God, which is in each and everyone of us, we can make a new start.

Right now God has need of all of you. You have unused talents and abilities. There are all kinds of possibilities before us, if we open our eyes to them. God is renewing in us the spirit of our minds so that we can rise up with a new spirit and take hold of life. We are in tune with the infinite, attuned to God's life and light.

The life of God heals and renews you. As I live each day in the rhythm and harmony of spirit, I am filled with joy. I live in love with life and its infinite possibilities. How beautiful to know that the almighty healing power, the life giving presence of God is right in the midst of us.

I am sure that during my by-pass operation spirit friends were present because I cannot remember leaving the ward or anything, until I woke up and yet my family say that I was talking to them.

When I am looking for words of comfort or answers to some problem I open my SNU hymn book. The one that I have chosen has no author but whoever wrote the words must have been truly inspired. Hymn number 314.

*Hand in hand with angels, through the world we go;*
*Brighter eyes are on us than we blind ones know;*
*Tenderer voices cheer us than we deaf will own;*
*Never, walking heavenward, can we walk alone.*

*Hand in hand with angels; some are out of sight;*
*Leading us unknowing into paths of light;*
*Some soft hands are covered from our mortal grasp,*
*Soul in soul to hold us with affirmer clasp.*

*Hand in hand with angels; walking every day,*
*How the chain may brighten none of us can say;*
*Yet it doubtless binds us, through the ties we love,*
*With the loftiest spirits in the realms above.*

*Hand in hand with angels ever let us go;*
*Clinging to the strong ones, drawing up the slow;*
*One electric love-chord, thrilling all with fire,*
*Soar we through vast ages, higher ever higher.*

God Bless.

# Spiritualism

ver the years I have come across several definitions of Spiritualism.

One said: Spiritualism is not a religion, it is revelation, a positive source of teaching which may exalt man to a higher understanding of truth and a purer worship and adoration of god.

Another read: Spiritualism is not a religion but a magnificent profession of truth, which carried all the responsibilities of religion.

In the book *The Arcana of Spiritualism* by Hudson Tuttle, it says: Spiritualism has no creed, for it cannot formulate a dogmatic system. It is the science of life, here and hereafter and is founded on facts. It regards belief without evidence as valueless.

Another definition says that Spiritualism is not a religion. It is the discovery of an actual fact in nature.

Like other facts in nature it has always existed and operated, even before it was discovered. It did not come into being just because it was discovered, any more than the continent of America came into being just because Columbus discovered it.

I also came across the statement that Spiritualism is a movement which differs from all others, for it began without a leader. It came into being under unusual circumstances simultaneously in different parts of the world. Abnormal manifestations of more or less identical nature occurred, which provoked attention, simulated investigations and the result spread far and wide.

The Spiritualist philosophy is of great importance which if followed will bestow countless blessings on those who practice it. We have a lot to live up to in our way of life – to realise how important our religion is – to accept responsibility. The greatest danger to the Spiritualist movement comes from those who speak for thrills or for self gain.

We have been given a wonderful jewel to take care of and we must not allow it to become tarnished or lose its brilliance. Let us all pull together to advance and make our presence felt, remembering that we are members of a spirit-guided movement.

Those who believe there is life after death of the physical body; that life is a an infinite prolongation and evolution of this; that the spirit remains unchanged in being and changes are only in conditions and that the spirit may hold communication with those in this life, are Spiritualists.

# Water from the Well

A short while ago I went to fill the kettle. I turned on the tap, and no water came out. What a surprise! When the water is turned off even for just a short time, we quickly clamour for the restoration of that precious fluid. I cannot remember how many times during that short period I went to the tap only to be disappointed. I said: "I wish we had a well in the garden."

If we think of a well we usually think of a deep hole in the ground containing water. The history of many countries of the world contains many references to wells and their great importance to life. The well was the public meeting place. I experienced this as a boy visiting relatives who lived in a village in Norfolk. The only supply of water was from the well. Here people met and exchanged thoughts and feelings.

In days gone by when local tribes were in conflict the natural target was the well. This was poisoned and usually brought quick submission from those residing there.

I could enumerate the blessings of water in many ways. It keeps us alive, it cleanses the body and grows our food. Every one of us can be likened to a well. It produces pure water, unless someone puts poison into it or stirs up the mud with in it.

We can only draw from the well of self what we allow to be drawn from us, so it is up to each and everyone to ensure that only pure thoughts and feelings are extracted when we go to this immortal well which holds, sustains and brings forth everything which is ever created.

Every human life is a force in this world. On every side our influences pour perpetually. If our lives are true and good, this influence is a blessing to other lives and we should never forget our joys are just as much required by the Great Spirit who charges the well with great love for our benefit. Spread the joys you receive from the well of life, for we must get our lives firmly attached to God if we are to draw from his fullness in time of need.

*God works in Mysterious Ways*
*His wonders to perform.*

# Life is for living

I recently heard someone say: "Life is for living." Right now is the time to enjoy life. I know that the past is gone and is but a memory and the future is yet to be but the present moment is the moment in which we are alive. It is at this present moment we may have to decide as to what our future might be.

As Spiritualists we should realise it is time to expand and express our spiritual powers and capabilities. Let us think of this present moment as a gift to use and appreciate. Everything we have are gifts that come from God. Let us think of life in terms of positive responses.

Let us accept the gifts of the present moment and re-dedicate ourselves to making it a rich and productive time. Whilst we may think with thankfulness of the blessings of the past, now we must fill our minds with positive thoughts of the future.

It is the present moment that offers us a new beginning and we can find life exciting and rewarding. We must learn to live in the present and life will have more meaning and we will enjoy it more.

Rejoice in the present moment, and live Life – one day at a time.

# The sea of life

On the first day of our holiday in Norfolk, we were greeted by a storm. Walking along the sea front in Cromer, chatting to the Lifeboat men, we were informed of the impending Force Nine gale rapidly rising. So we sought shelter in a café overlooking the sea. From the safety of our vantage point we watched the drama unfold. The waves racing towards the shore some as high as a house, lifting the pebbles, creating heaps all along the beach. The thought came to mind – 'the power of the sea'.

The next day was bright and sunny. I looked out to sea. It was now calm and sparkling blue. You would never believe the same sea could be so powerful; that it was responsible for all the damage along the coast when its calmness turned to storm. Yet has man not got the same elements in him as the sea? A calm and peaceful person can turn into a raging storm. We all have to experience the ocean of life. The ups and downs like the waves on the sea.

As I looked at the sea on that stormy day its colours were not that of a lovely blue but the dark colours of black and dark green, which again suggests that we, in the ocean of life do not have a life full of brightness all the time. That all must experience the darker colours so that when the storms of life are over, we experience the enlightenment.

As the sun comes out over life's ocean and brings back the brighter colours and a calmer sea, we can look forward and repair the damage that the sea of life has done. As I looked at that same beach, the calm sea lapping the shore, workmen were busy pushing the pebbles back, it was noticeable that the pebbles nearest to the sea were white from being in constant contact with it. But the further you looked towards the land the pebbles became greyer until they were very dark in colour. One could say it is the same with us who are in tune with God. Like the pebbles near to the sea we must never be out of touch with God.

A hymn written over a hundred years ago says:

> *Little drops of water,*
> *Little grains of sand*
> *Make the mighty ocean*
> *And the pleasant land.*

Little raindrops fall many miles away from the sea. Some are absorbed into the ground to keep alive the plant life on which we all depend. Others join together and make a stream which then joins with other streams and make a river. And we know that old man river goes rolling down to the mighty sea or ocean. We are the raindrops in this ocean of life. We join together in villages, towns, cities, clubs and churches, flowing, in different ways to join up in the great sea of life.

The drops of rain have different roles to play. As we have said, some give life to plants, others give us water to drink. Others go to make the all-powerful sea. We all know that at the end of our life, we go back to our beginning to start again the evolution of life, just as the raindrops evaporate into the atmosphere and make up the rain clouds to bring rain into the world again.

I have never enjoyed walking along the beach, but my wife loves to be on the sand or swimming in the sea. So on the next day of our holiday we went a little further along the coast to the seaside village of Overstrand. As we walked along the edge of the sea not wanting to get sand in my shoes, I gave in and took them off. Very quickly a wave moved forward and washed over my feet. As I felt its cooling balm I wondered where this life-giving water had been before it came here. I wondered how many miles it had travelled and how much turbulence it had been part of – this same water which now appeared so serene. We in the ocean of life will travel those same thousands of miles and experience much turbulence.

I stood and looked out to sea and wondered about other people on other shores, in far-away places over the sea. Looking into the sea I tried to consider how many generations, how many dynasties, how many civilizations it had travelled through. How many lives had been affected by its comings and goings and how many lives it had taken when it had lost its temper, the same sea here now with me, this caressing water that brushed over my feet.

It was soon gone, snatched back into the sea. I watched it go, knowing full well it would come back again in quiet patience or in a turbulent storm, to repeat its cycle; to wear away the rocks and carry the sand to other places. Living its life, doing its work and changing the very shape of the land – this gentle water washing my feet.

We, in this ocean of life, may have lived through many generations and civilizations. We may have affected others with our comings and goings. But we have to go on living our lives and doing our work until we are snatched away again.

The cruel sea – yes, we are just as the sea. We can erupt quickly from being calm and serene to be stormy tempest. Yet when our mood is calm, we, like the sea, can give an abundance of pleasure. Your life is just as the waves are. We get tossed around, but we know that a storm always blows itself out. Everything in the world starts small. Little acorns grow to be mighty oaks. The little drops of water run into streams and gather strength from others, move on and join other streams and gain more strength. They make a broad river which moves silently and slowly to join the ocean and here we can see the real power of little drops of water.

If we think of ourselves, we start off in life alone. Meeting other lives we gain experience and we are moved by others in the ocean of life. Some do well, like the raindrops that feed and water all life. Others flow to the ocean and use their strength pounding the rocks to no apparent useful end.

We cannot expect things to remain the same. We know that the tide changes but one thing we can be assured of is that the love of God is unchanging. We, in this life, must flow along with others who have good influences on us and, if we flow along with the good we will grow along with the good.

Next time you are standing looking out to sea just thank it for all the good things we harvest from it. For the pleasure it gives us and forgive its occasional loss of temper.

I particularly like the thoughts behind this poem:

*The Legend of the Raindrop*

*The legend of the raindrop has a lesson for us all,*
*As it trembled in the heavens, questioning whether it*
*should fall.*
*For the glistening raindrop argued to the genie in the sky,*
*I am beautiful and lovely as I sparkle here on high,*
*And hanging here I will become part of the rainbow's hue,*
*And I'll shimmer like a diamond, for all the world to view.*

*But the genie told the raindrop, Don't hesitate to go,*
*For you will be more beautiful, if you fall to earth below,*
*For you will sink into the soil, and be lost awhile from sight,*
*But when you reappear on earth, you will be looked on*
*with delight,*
*For you will be the raindrop, that quenched the thirsty ground,*
*And helped the lovely flowers, to blossom all around.*

*And in your resurrection, you'll appear in queenly clothes,*
*With the beauty of the lily, and the fragrance of the rose,*
*Then you will wilt and wither, and become part of the earth,*
*And make the soil more fertile, and give more flowers birth,*
*For there is nothing ever lost, or eternally neglected,*
*For everything God ever made, is always resurrected.*

*So trust God's all-wise wisdom, and doubt the Father never,*
*For in his heavenly kingdom, Nothing is lost forever.*

Helen Steiner Rice

# Responsibility

Barry Bishop National Geographic (1963)

In 1953 Edmund Hillary from New Zealand with a Sherpa called Tenzing Norgay accomplished what no other human beings ever had – they stood at the top of Mount Everest the world's highest peak. This was looked upon by all of the world as one of the greatest feats of endurance by human beings, for which Edmund Hillary was given a knighthood and while he accepted this honour he made it quite clear that he could not have succeeded without a team of good workers.

Tenzing tells the story of how for each level reached a high degree of teamwork was required. One group would exhaust themselves just getting the equipment up the mountain for the next group. Two groups of men worked finding a path, cutting steps and securing ropes; spending themselves to make the next leg of the climb possible for others.

You see, friends, you cannot climb a mountain like this by racing away on your own but slowly and carefully by unselfish team work. Everyone of us is trying to reach the top. It is the dream of everyone but I realise no one in any situation can reach it without the help of others.

Where would Hillary have been without the climbers who made the routes, the Sherpas who carried the loads and the people who cleared the paths ahead. It was only through the work and sacrifice of them all, working together, that they had a chance to reach the top.

When I was reading about Hillary my thoughts travelled back to the time when I worked underground as a miner. Here again is another example where the life of your comrade may depend on you. For as you work everything above you has to be made secure, there is no room to be unprofessional. Your skill, just like that of the Sherpa, may save someone's life. I had to make sure whoever followed me had faith and trust that I had prepared good conditions for him to be safe and secure.

In life I can say to you that you are on a pathway that has been prepared for you. Your father God is your Sherpa and you can put your trust in him.

If you follow in his footsteps you will sometimes find yourself in situations you do not understand but it is during these times, when you hold firmly to the truth, that you find he loves you as much on the bad days as he does on the good ones.

Many times on the mountain, climbers have good and bad days. They may slip and lose ground. They're afraid but they hold on to the life line and if the person whose job it was has made fast the hooks they will recover and get back on track.

Life is like a mountain and in life many fall by the wayside and find it hard to get back on track. We may look for help and feel there is no one there. Sometimes we put our trust in the wrong person or the wrong thing. Most of us are afraid that, if we accept ourselves, we are excusing all things that are wrong in us,

This is not so! Your father God who loves you will help you to correct yourself and remember God's correction is not a rejection or a disapproval of you.

I think what we have learned is that our lives revolve around our fifth principle 'Personal Responsibility'. A short version in the dictionary says: 'Responsibility is – the state, quality, or fact of being responsible, a thing or person that one is answerable for; a duty, obligation, or burden; being legally or ethically accountable for the care of others.'

I think you will agree that it takes special people to follow this definition. Let's look at it this way – God has given you the ability to choose your response. A short poem that I found says that:

*"Life is like a field of newly-fallen snow*
*Where I choose to walk every step will show."*

This sends us a message, a reminder, that we should set good examples for others to follow and show them we have left behind us a safe, secure path to be followed.

We have to thank our pioneers who cleared the pathways ahead of us so that we can be here today to follow our philosophy, free from persecution. They have passed that Responsibility to us. Are you prepared to make new pathways? For only through the work and sacrifice of us all working together as a team can we reach the top. For *teamwork* makes *dreams work*!

(written in 2004)

# On the move

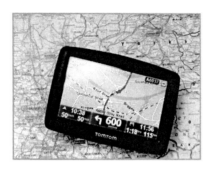

ravelling is something my wife Joyce and I have to do every week as we visit different churches and Her Majesty's Prisons – often for the first time. What used to be sometimes difficult journeys are now easier as we have a 'Sat-Nav'. Usually it ensures a stress-free route to our destination. However, despite the multitude of satisfied users, it is always the tiny minority of catastrophes that attract the attention of the press – reports that a motorist was directed to the top of a cliff and an articulated lorry sent down a country lane got stuck on a small bridge with a stream underneath.

The problem usually rises at the point that people opt to take the shortest route, on the mistaken premise it will make their journey shorter. The fact is that attempted short cuts can lead to disaster on all kinds of journeys whether they be material or spiritual.

Many times I have heard it said: "Oh how I would like to get away for a while and leave every thing behind." Their idea of course is to leave their worries and troubles locked up at home but you know that it is an impossible thing to do, as the troubles and worries are with them, and they will also travel. A troublesome illness would not be cured by taking it for a holiday but maybe the rest and the good sea air would ease the discomfort a little and offer a welcome respite.

From birth to death we are travelling on life's pathway – for some it may be a short journey for others the road could be hard and long.

Modern motorways have a number of lanes and it is for the user to choose the lane most suited to the particular vehicle in which they are travelling. There is of course a fast lane and many travellers never leave it. Maybe they arrive at their destination safely but statistics say that in time a mistake will happen and an accident will occur.

This also applies to travellers on life's highway. One can only use and abuse until disaster strikes. The story of the tortoise and the hare tells us that steady progress wins through and offers the best and easiest way. On life's highway there will be other users and sometimes they will hinder our progress. It is then we have to hold our thoughts and stay calm.

Right now we are on life's journey and, just like the motorway, there is more than one lane to travel in. While one may be easier than another, how we progress depends on a lot of reasons.

I am sure, like myself, you have taken the wrong way or missed the turn off and ended up on the wrong road. Sometimes it takes us out of our way and we have had to work our way back to where we wanted to be. Is not this the way of life? Many times we make the wrong choice, which takes our lives in a different direction and which may take time and effort to get back on track.

Sometimes in our life we get fed up of travelling light and take on more than we can cope with. We know that in the fast lane you can be pushed up to a speed where you find difficulty in keeping control. Isn't it true that peoples' attitudes can change when they get behind the wheel of a car?

On life's highway we have free-will to steer our lives in any direction we desire. Sometimes our life grinds to a halt but with help from other travellers we get restarted, just as on the highway – we only need a push to start up and move on.

Whatever journey we take in life we need to know what will guide us. We might be guided by the pursuit of money or fame. We might spend our time trying to achieve popularity, high status or perfect behaviour. Chasing these things will perhaps take us so far but they will not lead us to progress in the eternal life and a better relationship with God.

In a relationship with God we don't get to see life all mapped out but we can experience the presence of a personal guide. You must remember, to travel on a spiritual way of life is not an easy road. The demands on your life are many. You may find that your journey is hard and long and it is difficult to always stay on track. At the same time it is most important to realise that our will is in some ways like the machinery of a car. It is strong, efficient and powerful but it needs some other force to take hold, to switch on and fire it into life.

That is when we need a spirit helper near us ready to take hold of our lives and help us to find maximum power in our personality to be able to master the art of spiritual living.

I have just had a full service on my car. It did not come cheap but I know it has to be done if I want it to perform at its best. In the same way man must keep the machinery of the will in good repair. Let it, by discipline and endeavour, be efficient and strong and then let us learn how to supply it with the driving force which it needs if it is going to function adequately.

Interests, imagination, confidence are secrets we must understand – they flood the mind with feeling. Without them we are as those who laboriously push wheels around with their hands but when connected to the power of the spirit energies are released in the personality, greater than we ever dreamed of.

Modern life is full of breakdowns – not a good thing whether they take place on the road or within the human self. Sometimes it's just a small thing and does not take long to get going again but sometimes in life those who breakdown under the tremendous tasks and strains, which are often imposed on us in daily life, may need to have more attention to get back on the road again.

Remember, recovery is on hand, travel with confidence, place your trust in God and may your journey be full of spiritual progress.

# Nature

It is our duty as Spiritualists to bring into our daily lives the highest ideals possible but the nature of man is more material than spiritual, although occasionally we allow the divinity within us to come to the surface.

I realise there are so many things in this world crying out for our attention that our life is planned around material pleasure and it requires persistent efforts to allow the spiritual side of ourselves to function normally and naturally.

Our dominant thoughts are so crowded by events and happenings in our daily lives that the clear insight of the spiritual self does not get a chance to reveal the silent truth awaiting our acceptance. Nevertheless the impelling soul which lies at the centre of life will always urge and prompt us through that still small voice within.

Meditation, contemplation and the disciplining of the mind and heart will allow the central spiritual force to awaken and gradually reveal itself. Nothing is more important than the daily thought of allowing the God-within to be ever present in our mind and heart. Spiritualised consciousness is not always detrimental in our objective life, because whatever our occupation or profession a spiritual state of mind will enhance it.

We may ask how we may achieve this spiritualised state of mind each day. Bringing God and the divine intelligences into our lives means that our first waking thoughts each morning should be to give thanks to God, with a prayer of gratitude and a humble request to be guided and to be the means of serving the needs of others.

Before you make any decision or take any important action offer a prayer for guidance that your actions may be blessed by your Father God.

Before you speak or carry out some important task, allow yourself, for just a few seconds, to become aware of the spiritual consciousness within and you will find a source of inspiration peace and a calm that you little realized was available to you.

Seek always to improve your character, and to emulate the highest ideals of thought and conduct. Never feel you cannot achieve your aims, but realise that the divine consciousness will grow stronger each moment of each day and will always be present so that you may truly reflect the fullness and beauty of your own divinity. With love and harmony, the result will be the presence of God in your daily life.

If we are true believers in the good we would want to share our treasures but how do we encourage people to be good in this day and age? We must advertise the strength of the spirit. We must not show the weaknesses of self. Envy and jealousy must not be seen in Spiritualists. We, as Spiritualists, should understand life far better than any other religion for we know that, even though we may lose everything in this life, we have the knowledge and joy that we 'live on' after death.

The importance of being here is to increase our good efforts; to turn everything in our lives to good. All our thoughts and actions must be pure, to instil a balance of sanity in the world.

This is a task that is awaiting us as Spiritualists. We must create a world where everyone can live in harmony and peace. Radiate your spiritual life and express peace and love from within by sharing your thoughts with those who need them. Unite your thoughts and actions and work together in spreading this great truth, for this is your heritage – guard it, fight for it, for there are many who would take it away and destroy it.

Your understanding of God must grow, at least in proportion to your increased knowledge, to help the people who are looking to Spiritualism for a new way of life. People of other religions realise, as we have, that their ideas are now obsolete. We must help them find a new way of life with the knowledge of life after death, because if we rob them of that they have nothing left.

We are all seeking love, and love comes in many different ways. God's love is important and God loves you no matter how unimportant you think you are. Regardless of how wrongly you think you have handled anything in your life, God loves you and you do not have to measure up to anyone else's expectations. God will not punish us. How can we believe that of a

God of love? But that does not mean that you go scot free.

Some people say there is no God, that nature rules the world. Let me take you for a walk that I went on with my father.

Let us for a few moments imagine a lovely sunny day and that you are sitting beside a pond, everything is perfect. Dad would say: "Look into the water, in there are things that the eyes cannot see, flies, bugs." We'd look into the reeds; sitting there, motionless, a large frog; we'd see insects skimming across the water. Then he told us that they have all got one thing in common – to kill and devour or escape from being devoured. Yes, the pond is a battlefield. Why is nature so designed? Each creature depends for its food by killing another – in what is known as a food-chain. This is the design – the plan within nature – each one supporting the whole system. But if this 'survival' is the only plan, where can we find a guide for just living?

In some ways this world is akin to the pond, but we must place the scales of justice on a different plane of conscience.

Too many in this our world live by preying on the weak and crawling away from the strong in their system. We cannot live like this. We need to build a life worth living. We must motivate our inner self and bring the God-self into our daily lives. Sometimes we are called upon to make the best of some situation that may call for all the courage, strength and faith we possess.

We all know of someone who has made the best of a bad situation or illness and we were impressed by their remarkable efforts; people in all kinds of situations who carry on and remake their lives. People who have illnesses or afflictions must have help from the strong but in all things people have to work together for good.

The gist of this lesson is that God is light, peace and love; God is strength and harmony. The truth is that he is our protection at all times. Always we have God's love to guide us; the love of God to protect us. We never need to feel alone or insecure, for God is with us wherever we are and whatever we do.

*How doth the little busy bee*
*Improve each shining hour,*
*And gather honey all the day*
*From every opening flower.*
*Isaac Watts*

# Think positive!

How many times have you heard the saying – 'Think positive'?

We are told that we must at all times – 'think positive thoughts' and that those thoughts are living things.

This is not something new, for this phrase is used in every book that has been written on personal development. It goes back in ancient writings and can be found in the scriptures of the bible in one form or another. So why is it that we all need to be told time and time again to order our thoughts? I suppose the answer is quite simple, most of us have not yet mastered the thought process we engage in every moment of our lives.

It is said – 'as a man thinketh so he becomes'. We must realise that we all are at this moment creating our future by the fabric of our thoughts. We can transform the lives of those around us by the thoughts we send in their direction, so take a good look at your thinking pattern and ask yourself – how positive and beneficial your thinking is. Are the thoughts you create supportive of life? Do your thoughts uplift and inspire you to do better things?

Remember thoughts create feelings, therefore the way you feel is determined by the way you think.

One of the most important changes we can make is to start loving ourselves. That might seem selfish, but in loving ourselves and all our fellow men, we begin to love that which our world can give us freely and lovingly. Then we can appreciate more and more the things we take for granted, the things we fail to notice and fail to understand. Are you willing to forget what you have done for other people and remember what people have done for you? Can you ignore what the world owes you and think what you owe the world?

Remember there are no superhumans. Successful people are those who have developed a strong belief in themselves through a positive way of thinking.

# The play goes on

very Christmas brings thoughts of Christmases past. The tradition of Christmas is still carried on in our family. The play goes on, but the players have changed, some are no longer with us and new lives have taken their places.

As I write I find myself thinking about my mother, who at ninety years old suddenly decided that her part in this life was over and passed into spirit. Now we had to take over. The family needed a new leader. Someone must take over the leading role.

Not an easy task to follow such a great lady. She was gifted in speech and song, shrewd and far-seeing, had a knowledge of many subjects and, yes, a faith that could move mountains.

When I received my 'call up' papers for the armed forces my mother gave me a card on which she had written these words: "Man can plan but God will decide." Many times in my life these words were proved true.

Her last words to us were that she loved us and we told her that we loved her.  Love – the almighty link. How can anyone die? We all need love, we must have love, we pray for love, and believe in love. We must love ourselves and inspire others to love one another. It is love that builds our philosophy of life along the right lines.

Spiritualism, as we know it, is not going along to the local church in hope of a message from the spirit world. No! It's more than that. Spiritualism is a philosophy for life – for living, for dying, and for what follows physical death and it all is based on love for one another.

*A junior school Christmas collage*

# Searching

ovies and TV often show heroes having incredible adventures exploring in space; rediscovering lost cities; finding a way out of some impossible situation or saving the world from destruction.

The actors, who play these parts, have us spellbound and bring a real excitement into our lives.

This is how you should feel when you enter your church, for there you will find that is where excitement unfolds. It is tangible and far more exciting and interesting than any film plot. You are in a place where you can receive directions that will elevate you. We do not demand that you believe without question. We are seekers of the truth. Use your own observation and understanding and listen carefully to the philosophy given from the platform – some speakers are more experienced than others.

Evaluate with an open mind; observe and investigate; decide if this way of life is right for you; reach your own conclusion. Remember evaluated experiences lift you above the crowd.

People who make it a practice to reflect on their experiences and learn from them are rare, the truth is that experience is costly, you cannot gain experience without paying a price and hopefully you get value for the price that you pay.

We believe that death is merely the disintegration of the physical body and there is an after-life for the spirit or soul which continues living. Those who have strong bonds with relatives or friends left on earth will sometimes communicate with them through mediums. Spiritualists are continually explaining to non-Spiritualists that we cannot demand contact with those who have passed on. It is those in the spirit world who wish to return. You cannot command help from the spirit world, all you can do is to put yourself in the right condition to receive it. When you are spiritually ready, the higher power will reach you. Never forget that you are essential to the scheme. You were born with all the equipment needed mentally, physically and spiritually, for this life, provided by your God as part of your divine heritage. It is up to you to use them.

The purpose of this life is that the good within should control and dominate your life. The things of the spirit are found in the warm simple way of life, in love and human kindness. In this way we can create a Brotherhood of all people. As we become more sensitive and aware of the spirit around us, we will notice by our thoughts, speech and actions that we have progressed. If we pursue this way of life we will find then the true meaning of love and then endeavour to inspire by example, which is to search for and encourage good ideas coming from the world of spirit.

I was told at a young age that patience was a virtue. There are great benefits in waiting. For example if you learn to wait and observe you will make better choices. I like to see my garden neat and tidy, but I'm slow at getting the inspiration to change to perspiration. My great ideas don't become reality because I don't spend time and energy to make them happen. I realise that if I don't cultivate life's garden it also will suffer and not look its best.

Everything we grow, be it material or spiritual, needs our best efforts if we want the best fruits of our labours. With perseverance and regular practice this spiritual inspiration will gradually give rise to an abiding inward tranquillity, which will impart strength and love to the soul where ever it goes. The peace of the garden will unfold it and from the emotions, purified and blessed by the spirit, will flow out and enfold those in need of sympathy and healing.

We must not be ignorant of our true being. The earthly body is not permanent for it passes away at the end of this mortal life. Whilst we live on earth most people never give it a thought and may never know of the more important body which remains unseen to the human eye, though ever-present around us all.

Being spiritual and of finer substance than material things it is not seen by normal vision, but, be assured, it is there nevertheless.

This is our 'real body' for therein dwells the life and the true personality with all its attributes and at death is disassociated from the physical form to enter a life more real and without end.

The so-called 'death', dreaded by many, is but the natural escape of the living spirit, from the bonds of its earthly covering and will evolve into a world of greater activity.

All of us are spirit with everlasting life, for such is in accordance with the divine plan and no one can evade it. Those who prove faithful here will have a place of responsibility in the world of spirit. Knowing this ought to give us true purpose in our lives in this world. Our eternal honour and employment will depend upon the way we have conducted ourselves in this life.

Life is a continuous and expanding process. The purpose of this life is to build a character that is fitting for the next part of your life's journey. These are the 'school days' of the spirit. Learn your lessons well so that you can move into the greater existence beyond and you can then always rise higher because you will be in a world of eternal progress. Spiritualism is a science, a philosophy and a religion. A way of life all in one. Your life is the growth of the spirit, into the whole being. Be aware of the beauty and goodness in God's world, for many times the heavenly messengers come bringing us heavenly blessings but we are so intent on earthly things that we do not see them or open the door to them.

If we would but train ourselves to be more aware of those spirit friends who accompany us through life then, when they knock on the door, we will be ready to give a loving welcome. The parallel to life on earth is profound. It really does not make any difference how the world ranks your status, because the fact of your birth gives you a divine heritage. All noble life must be inspired by the spirit. We must seek the brightest and the best to work with.

A good motto for life is – Live for immortal things.

*A winter's morning.*

*Trees*

*The trees in winter stand*
*So bleak and bare,*
*But beneath the ground the roots are feeding*
*New life to prepare.*

*In spring the buds are beautiful*
*With nature's love and care*
*They bring with them the promise*
*Of a world so fair.*

*The buds they burst in summer*
*Bringing shades of green.*
*They stand in all their glory*
*A pleasure to be seen.*

*Autumn sees the turning of the leaves*
*From green to brown*
*Falling in their numbers*
*Heaped upon the ground.*

*Why has all this happened?*
*Is a question you can ask.*
*This is one of nature's lessons*
*Have you begun to grasp?*

*The leaf has served its purpose*
*It falls upon the ground*
*But it will return again*
*And pleasure will abound.*

*S Pickersgill*

# Experience diversity

The seed of all life lies in the dark until it is time to waken and then, after the trials and tribulations through the growing pains of experience, just when we think we know how to handle it, we have discouraging times when things don't go well for us – when everything seems to go wrong. How should it be otherwise? For if we could go through life easily, what would be the point? The storms and dark clouds, which are life's winter can only be pointers to the brighter and happier days of summer. Should your path of life now be clouded with pain and unhappiness, realise that we grow under the apparent darkness of what we consider our disadvantages. Do not despair for they may turn out to be our most indispensable advantages.

We all have hidden, undeveloped characters. We all have powers which we have barely begun to exercise. Everyone at some time or another begins to question the purpose of life. Some come into our churches, and there we can teach them that by being patient and developing the inner-self (the true-self) pointers to the future are given.

We often find that circumstances of life have either set us on a course that we have to travel, or by some unknown chance we have been guided on to a desired path which our inspirers intended us to walk. Some schools of thought say that our destinies are planned out for us and whether we like it or not we automatically go the way allotted to us. Others say that man is a free agent and the master of his own fate. So, we have a diversity of opinion but as the seasons change we see that there is ever much beauty in diversity, whether a tiny flower or a majestic tree, the smallest gem or the highest snow covered mountain.

Truth, like a diamond, has many facets and can be viewed from all angles, so no man can say he possesses the whole truth. The final truth is beyond the understanding of all human beings and is the quest of our eternal journey once we have left this earth.

*After the storm*

# Don't fret!

When I wrote this I felt very privileged that God had given me another chance. I was lying in a hospital bed, wondering what the future would be. I looked around and could see there were others worse than me. There were six beds and no one was in a talkative mood, each allowing thoughts to dwell on self.

One day after a short sleep, I woke to find a patient sitting at my bedside and he asked how I was. He told me that he had had a stroke which had left him without the use of his right hand. "Can you fasten my buttons for me?" he asked. I did and from then on we were mates.

He helped me to forget myself. He had a saying for when things went wrong – "Don't fret about it." This made me think of the many things that we do fret about. We often worry about things that have not turned out as we had wished and if we allow fretting to become a habit we waste time and energy on things we can do nothing about.

Never fret about the weather – we cannot alter it; never fret about people – you cannot change them. Try not to fret about the little things that crop up in your daily life. When you joined a queue and it seems to take the longest time to move; when you are about to cross the road and there are no gaps in the traffic fretting is futile, wasteful, and destructive. It will wear you out.

When you find yourself worrying about the future just stop and let your thoughts stand still in this precious moment here with you now.

The past has gone and is a memory and the future is yet to be. So thank God for today and do not worry about tomorrow. Live life to the full; seize and use every opportunity large or small; rise to every challenge and make the utmost of what it offers; make a clean sweep of all your worries. Then fill the empty spaces with positive belief in God's ability to handle your affairs.

Your prayers each morning should be: "Please God, do not let anything happen to me today that you and I cannot handle together."

# Life changing

If only life was like a film set, we could keep repeating certain parts of our life that we enjoyed. If we got things wrong we could keep trying again and again, until we got them right. If we get our words wrong we can say them over and over until we become word perfect.

If only life was like a film set – any mistakes that take place on the set can be corrected before the viewing audience gets to see the film. All the director has to do is to shout, "Cut!" and ask the actors to repeat the scene until it is perfect. If a line is forgotten or a dance routine ruined, it doesn't matter, the actors can do it again and again until the finished piece is flawless.

If only life was like that we could repeat certain parts of our life until we got them right. If we had spoken out of turn we could rewind until we were word perfect – but it's not. In life there are no short cuts, no extra takes, life is a live show not a rehearsal. We make mistakes, words slip out in the wrong place, some of our moves put us and others in a bad light.

We are all on stage in the theatre of life. Sometimes it will be a comedy which may include errors.

It may be a drama that is happy for some but sad for others or it could be a sporting life of excitement and making front page news Perhaps it is an adventure in far away places, which could include a romance.

Remember you may be in the spot light – what part are you playing? Is it a show stopping performance, winning awards, recognised and respected for what you do? As adults we have responsibilities, pressures, relationships and finances that need managing. Some days things go well. On others we feel bogged down with troubles so it's no surprise that we wish we could rewind our lives and start again.

Help is on hand. Your Father God is in the director's chair, he will support and guide you and under his guidance you can become a new character – there could be a choice of a spiritual part requiring dedication.

The true fact is that God is more interested in who you really are than in what you do in terms of work and skill. God is more interested in the person than in their ability. Therefore we all can be ambassadors if we truly manifest the power and the fruits of the spirit.

Remember when God gives you an assignment, he will give you all that is needed to fulfil it. What is needed is your devotion; in fact by studying your competencies you can actually discern your calling.

Winston Churchill said: "To each there comes in his or her lifetime a special moment when they are tapped on the shoulder and offered the chance to do a very special thing, unique to them and fitted to their talent." But at that moment perhaps we find that we are unprepared for that which could have been our finest hour.

You cannot be all you want to be but you can be all that God wants you to be, if he is the director in your life. We all have different gifts but it is the spirit who helps and guides us.

Every one of my age grew up with the comic books full of heroes. Every week I looked forward to Superman, someone who could change very quickly by just popping into a telephone box and Clark Kent came out in that wonderful attire of Superman, his personality changed. On the other hand if it was the Incredible Hulk, it was some special moment that triggered him to change his appearance which made him into something special. There were others like Batman and Robin, Spiderman and Wonder Woman, who were there if there was a crisis or an emergency and if they were in pursuit of a criminal, they always 'got their man'. The super-heroes were always depicted as ordinary people just like you or me who could change; I suppose it would be something if we could just pop into the next room and become someone special.

Who would you be?

But then I'm sure you know that you are special to your friends and loved ones and more even more special to God just by being the best that you can.

# Friendship

A word we use a lot in our church service is 'friend'. When you come to think of it the greatest things in the universe are old mountains, old rivers, old seas and old stars. This is true in the realms of human life, where old friends are the greatest prized of them all.

What is a friend? Thousands of books have been written and as many speakers have delivered talks and sermons on the wonders of friendship. Like all wonderful things, true friendships are rare, and things that are rare are difficult to obtain or explain.

What must we look for in friendship? Like good wine, friendship must be cultivated patiently by sincerity, frankness and deeds of affection. Have you ever thought that if you had not been friends with a certain person, your life would have been different in many ways? I know that mine would!

Certain of my friends have made me see things differently and have modified my outlook. They have enlarged my horizons and given me new ideas. Good friends influence us far more than we realize. With friends we also experience suffering when our friends suffer.

Friendship gives us confidence in life and in ourselves. If we had to lose everything in this life but still have one friend, life would still be bearable. We know without argument that friendship depends on confidence and trust and if they are undermined, that friendship is broken. Those who cannot give friendship will rarely receive it and never hold it.

If your friendship has not come up to your expectations, search your heart and ask yourself, have you been a true friend? For friendship is a two-way thing but one of the consolations of real friendship is that they are not only for this life. We have friends in spirit who will, if we allow, look after our well-being and personal progress in life.

*Relativity*

*There was a young lady named Bright,*
*Who travelled faster than light.*
*She started one day,*
*In the relative way,*
*And came back the previous night.*

# The Architect

When an Architect plans a building, he has to know what weight-load the foundation will carry and the kind of storms the building will have to face.

God is the architect of people, of you and me, and when he builds he empathises foundations. He knows what weight-load you and I will be called on to carry and what kind of storms we will have to face, so he lays our foundations accordingly.

Can you look at yourself and say you did a good job. If you can't then maybe there is a need for some restoration. If we neglect the foundations even the most expensive building will fall, so we must make sure our lives are built on spiritual foundations.

We know that every condition starts with a foundation and right now we are laying the foundations for the future. What we do in this life will determine our status in the next. You were put on this earth to make a contribution. You were not created to consume resources, just to eat, breathe and take up space – you were placed on earth to make a difference. Everyone of us therefore is essential and valuable. We are all unique individuals and as Spiritualists we are an indispensable part of God's creation.

At times circumstances – and people – seem to be pushing us beyond that which we can bear but God knows our limitations and he never allows any difficulties to enter our lives that exceed our strength and ability to endure. Every human being has a work-load limit which varies from person to person. Some people for example can bear the pressure better than others and yet everyone has a breaking point. It is then when we have to know how much stress the foundations will hold.

There maybe someone in your life who is silently carrying a problem, a huge weight of mind, and although they are crumbling under the load they battle on. People who tend and care for family and loved ones with disabilities or illness over a long period of time must be such special individuals and are of great value. There is an unseen source of help from which we can take courage when facing a physical or spiritual crisis. Our ministering spirits are around us helping and inspiring us. Little do we know of the powerful help and protection they provide. You may say I have never seen spirit. I say there is no need. It's enough to know that they also battle on silently and do their work beyond the realms of physical sight. Just to know that these unseen helpers are on our side can strengthen us and our trust in God.

We have all seen load limit signs on highway bridges. Engineers determine the exact amount of stress that various materials can safely endure, as they know that too much strain can cause severe damage or complete collapse. So the posted warnings tell us not to exceed the maximum load. Each and every one of us, like the bridge, has a load limit. Some people can take the strain better than others but everyone has a breaking point. This I know.

*When sorrow assails us or terror draws nigh,*
*His love will not fail us, he'll guide with his eye,*
*And when we are fainting and ready to fail*
*He'll give what is lacking and make us prevail.*

It is said that the higher the building the deeper the foundations must be. The most important part of any building are the foundations. Without a solid base the edifice is at risk of cracking and crashing to the ground. Whenever a powerful earthquake hits a region with a result in a large loss of life and the destruction of an number of buildings, many investigations too often reveal that the construction company have cut corners. The foundations were neglected, with the result the building could not withstand the force of the quake.

So no matter what you are trying to build, be it a business, a ministry or a relationship, give it time to grow if you want it to survive. Remember too, to build your spiritual lives with strong foundations, knowing that we have the mind of spirit and need to allow this to function through us to change our whole life and thoughts.

I believe that we evolve our character and personality while we are here on earth, we cannot cheat. On arriving in the next dimension of life, every thought, every deed arrives with us. However circumstances of the life we have lived are taken into consideration. Sometimes what we thought was bad is seen in a different light. We may judge ourselves harshly but there will be the opportunity to progress, by serving those less fortunate than ourselves and who knows perhaps we will be on a higher level of progression than we ever imagined.

Remember we are all part of God's house. He uses each and every one of us and if we want to be a part, what would you be?

A foundation or a corner stone that holds the building together? If we decide to take that part, then we must stand out with confidence. A well-maintained building stands out in the community so we must build a strong character and have integrity, and that requires that you be consistent and sound in your values, thoughts, and actions.

Your life is a story and each day you get to write a new page, so fill those pages in with integrity – with responsibility, to God, to others and to yourself. If you do this you will not be disappointed.

## Words

Words we speak them every day
giving little thought to what we say,
speak them casually or with feeling.
Sometimes hurting, sometimes healing.

The tone we use conveys a great deal,
according to the way we feel,
in times of grief cannot find any,
other times we say far too many

Words can put you on the rack,
often in no position to answer back.
They can become an invisible foe,
peace destroyed with an unseen blow.

Silence is golden it is said,
Before you break it – think instead.

(Author unknown)

# About the Author

Sidney Pickersgill was born in 1931 in a small mining village near Wakefield in Yorkshire. His father, a miner, was a staunch Methodist, mother a Salvationist and Sid sang in the local church choir.

He attended local schools until at the age of fourteen he began work in the local boot and clog factory. Following four years of National Service in the army, where he was kept at 'Base' because of his skills in repairing equipment, he returned to the factory but soon joined his friends down the local coal mine, where the pay was better.

Four years later, seeking a better life for his growing family they emigrated to Australia but returned, for family reasons, after only three years. He later met and married Joyce and they brought up his family of three boys together.

His first love has always been healing, becoming a member of Castleford healing group in 1960. He later transfered to Wakefield Spiritualist Church and has been a member for over fifty years, serving as secretary and then, for seventeen years, as President. He now holds the title of Honorary President and has the long service award of the Spiritualists' National Union.

As a Prison Chaplain he visits the local prisons.

Sid and Joyce both hold the Healing diploma of the SNU, working in church and also attending hospitals.

Lightning Source UK Ltd.
Milton Keynes UK
UKOW051016270212

187994UK00001B/24/P